# BEYOND BONDING

◆ ◆ ◆

## A THIRD WORLD WOMEN'S THEOLOGICAL JOURNEY

**Virginia Fabella, M.M.**

Ecumenical Association of
Third World Theologians
and the
Institute of Women's Studies

# BEYOND BONDING

◆ ◆ ◆

A Joint Publication of the **Ecumenical Association of Third World Theologians** and the **Institute of Women's Studies**

©1993 Manila, Philippines

Book Design: IgeRamos
Production: Tomato Graphics Design Service Bureau
Printing: Excel Printing Services

Text set in Garamond Book. Titles and Headings set in Futura Condensed and its variants, encoded on Aldus PageMaker 4.2 Macintosh Version by Tomato Graphics

ISBN - 971-8605-12-6

# CONTENTS

**FOREWORD**                                 **VII**

INCLUSIVE AND LIBERATIVE FOR ALL
by Mercy Amba Oduyoye

**INTRODUCTION**                                 **1**

The Need for the Study
Clarification of Terms
Overview of the Chapters
Expectations and Acknowledgments

**CHAPTER ONE**                                 **7**

A MOVEMENT NAMED EATWOT

The Decade before EATWOT's Birth
The Responses to "Underdevelopment"
The Roots of EATWOT
The Beginnings of EATWOT
The Dar es Salaam Experience Assessed

**CHAPTER TWO**                                 **21**

EATWOT'S FIRST FIVE YEARS

EATWOT's Initial Five-Year Program
The Delhi Experience
"The Irruption within the Irruption"
EATWOT's Achievements

**CHAPTER THREE**                                 **33**

THE EATWOT WOMEN'S COMMISSION

The Setting
The Birthing Process
Implementing the Program
Organizing the Continental Consultations

**CHAPTER FOUR**         **47**

    THE "OAXTEPEC ENCOUNTER" AND AFTER

        The Women's Double Preparation
        The Oaxtepec Encounter
        EATWOT's Oaxtepec Assembly
        After Oaxtepec

**CHAPTER FIVE**         **67**

    EATWOT WOMEN:
    THEIR OWN THEOLOGICAL JOURNEYS

        African Women's Stories
        Latin American Women's Stories
        Asian Women's Stories
        Comparing the Women's Journeys

**CHAPTER SIX**         **91**

    EATWOT WOMEN EN ROUTE

        Different but Similar
        Similar but Different
        The Influence of Context
        The Function of Methodology
        The Role of EATWOT

**CHAPTER SEVEN**         **109**

    CHARTING THE FUTURE

        Twelve Findings
        Recommended Tasks for the Future
        Implications for the Future

**AFTERWORD**         **115**

    THE JOURNEY CONTINUES

**NOTES**         **119**

**SOURCES CONSULTED**         **147**

# FOREWORD

## INCLUSIVE AND LIBERATIVE FOR ALL

By writing *Beyond Bonding: A Third World Women's Theological Journey*, Virginia Fabella has once again pioneered and empowered women theologians in the Third World. The book tells the story of the women members of the Ecumenical Association of Third World Theologians (EATWOT). Eight months before EATWOT was inaugurated Fabella was already working for it and laying the foundation on which to build the membership of women in the Association. That women became members of EATWOT was in itself no mean achievement for either the women or the Association. The image of "a theologian" did not fit well with being a woman, so women theologians took on the demeanor and stance of the men who were their teachers and colleagues. Thus until the assembly in New Delhi in 1981 which marked EATWOT's fifth anniversary there was no specific word from women. Women were "peripheral or supplementary."

Fabella is writing an aspect of EATWOT's history and ministry that will ensure that women are not absent in this chronicle as has been the case in traditional historiography relating to the Church and its ministry. She herself states that this is no objective piece of scientific writing. She is a participant observer using scientific analysis to put on paper the processes that have yielded theological publications by EATWOT women. EATWOT women are by no means the only women theologians in the world, but this deliberate choice is made to tell the story of how, in the context of EATWOT, Third World women's theological consciousness developed. As the first woman executive secretary of the Association and a key architect of EATWOT's Women's Commission whose activities feature so prominently in this work, her decision to withhold her own story is regretted. Originally written as her doctoral dissertation entitled, "The Development of Women's Theological Consciousness within the Ecumenical Association of Third World Theologians," the book employs the academic third person, but as one who participated with her in the pre-Delhi days, I read every "they" as "we" and relive this history with astonished joy.

It is interesting how most of the "personal" histories recounted in chapter five parallel the corporate journey. Fabella captures the growth from so-called universal theology through attempts at doing theology relevant to the context, to a differentiation in the various foci for liberation, specifically a theology promoting a full life not only for women but for the entire human community and the whole of creation. Focusing on a geographical Third World which is here limited to Africa, Asia, and Latin America, with their shared historical context of colonialism and neocolonialism, Fabella maps out not only the similarities in the theologies in EATWOT but also the differences. Having been in all major EATWOT events, Fabella is eminently suited for giving us this inside story and much of what lies behind the growing library of EATWOT-related writings, which, until New Delhi, were mostly nurtured by men theologians. Fabella*is* part of EATWOT history.

A high mark for EATWOT women was New Delhi, where they woke up to five years of marginalization. They began to assert that there is a "liberative alternative" to what the men were proposing, and that women need special space and power within EATWOT to explore their visions and perspectives. The vivid story told in chapter two of EATWOT's first five years gives birth to the Women's Commission in chapter three. This chapter and the next are pivotal to any attempt at understanding the extent and depth and quality of participation of women in EATWOT. It makes the Nairobi assembly in 1992 sound like a backlash when Fabella points out that the original four major speakers chosen for the assembly were all men while women were "co-opted" as respondents. It is interesting to note that apart from the formal speeches presented by the men, the rest of the assembly process was heavily influenced by women. Fabella rightly observes that the issue here is partnership if EATWOT is serious about a more inclusive Third World theology.

Through the years of the first phase of the Women's Commission—from Delhi to Oaxtepec—women expanded the liberation methodology of EATWOT, adding the analysis of women's reality.

Here Fabella comments on aspects that need further attention like language, the grid of class, gender and race, and the aggravation of it all by a lack of caring towards creation. The inclusiveness sought by women demands a comprehensive analysis of the global reality. Fabella touches here a very crucial factor, as resisting sexism and racism is a central factor to the lives of women who are black. It is a theme that touches on solidarity among women and promises to be a real challenge even within the sisterhood of EATWOT and more especially when we seek dialogue and concerted action against patriarchy with our First World sisters.

The tension between acknowledging global sisterhood and "doing our own thing" as Third World women is highlighted by Fabella's criticism that "they have not made much use of the feminist theories in their gender analysis." Third World women's liberation theology stands between Third World men and Western feminists and womanists. While we create "a new thing" and are anxious not to be classified as aping Western women, we see the affinity and need to honor the work done in its context. The same goes for the men's theology in the Third World. Both this and "the language" challenge make fascinating reading and will certainly generate debate within and outside EATWOT. This tension is not only between Third and First World women. There is tension among ourselves as Third World women, and even on the continental level there are tensions and divergences. In a caring context all these are seen as positive for growth and appropriated as such. Even the explosion of the unacknowledged tension between EATWOT women and EATWOT men at New Delhi was appropriated in a creative way both in the birth of the Women's Commission and in the gradual appropriation of women's perspectives by EATWOT men, coupled with the generation of mutual respect. "Openness among the men to dialogue with the women on women's issues" is gradually replacing the "condescending and trivializing behavior of the past," says Fabella. Recording this healing ministry will hopefully serve to promote a common EATWOT agenda that faces patriarchy as the "system that keeps all forms of oppression intact" and enable the whole of EATWOT "to consider the feminist vision as an alternative political vision."

Although the development of theological themes is not central to the work, Fabella shows how the women's projects of revisiting Christology and spirituality have had repercussions on the programs of EATWOT, while illustrating how "context influences not only the focus of the women's theological tasks but the content of their reflection as well." At the same time she brings out the differences occasioned by the diverse contexts, experiences, exposure and involvement in other movements and praxis and most important, in learning to do collective theology. Unlike the pre-Delhi women members of EATWOT, most of the "younger" ones come to EATWOT with a conscious women's agenda, having been attracted to EATWOT through the work of the Women's Commission. They have not had to experience the situation in which "males asked the questions, supplied the answers, developed the method, and determined the framework," even when they talked about women. No longer will EATWOT women open themselves "to co-optation in theology" whether from Western women or from Third World men.

The conclusions and recommendations in chapter seven follow the hermeneutical cycle of liberation methodology. Those who have read or would take time to read the literature referred to by Fabella cannot but agree with her that "Third World women are no longer voiceless or invisible in the theological world." We are saying our own word as well as reflecting further on the words we have uttered and the praxis related to the word. Fabella's twelve findings in this chapter lead to further efforts to become more relevant and effective in the theological enterprise and in serving the mission of God. She points out that doing theology is "a specific way of struggling for life." It is, in fact, "in itself a ministry, and not a separate marginal activity." To be adequate to this ministry, Fabella calls attention to future tasks which derive from her conclusions. The call is to follow this program, not simply by stirring the soup pot but by discovering new ingredients. We are called to creativity as we analyze and reflect on our context and as we read and reread the Bible. Surely it is a long journey but the first step has been taken and encouraged by an Akan saying: "However long the journey, it ends at the door step." I commend this communal journey to you all.

This historical narrative makes EATWOT women aware of where they are coming from and where they are striving to go:

Our people's mythic/religious, historical and cultural context.

The seemingly indelible stains of colonial heritage.

The presence of the chameleon called neocolonialism.

The resistance and the struggles for transformation.

The earth and its environment whose groaning fills our ears.

This is the context of Third World women theologians. For EATWOT women, this is the context for commitment to a liberative praxis and a relevant theology and liturgy and spirituality—a ministry to bring the reality of the gospel into human affairs. The book's title *Beyond Bonding* is apt. As EATWOT women it is urgent that we move "beyond bonding" if our commitment is to bear fruit that will remain. Setting the story of our theological journey down in a way that more can have access to will certainly help to further the processes that the Women's Commission has set for itself, and please God, influence the two groups of theologians—our First World sisters and Third World brothers—between whom we stand.

**Mercy Amba Oduyoye**
Geneva, 10 February, 1993

# INTRODUCTION
◆ ◆ ◆

The work of contextualizing theology in the Third World has been underway for the past few decades.  In Africa, Asia, and Latin America, as well as in other parts of the globe, Christian theologians are taking their context seriously not only as a valid starting point but also as a determining factor in the reformulation of theology. Liberation theology in Latin America, minjung theology in Korea, and black theology in South Africa, are among the emergent contextual theologies that have arisen out of people's real life experience and the concrete and urgent problems that beset them.

One flaw in the process is the absence or mere token presence of women's perspective and contribution.  While Third World women have begun to reflect theologically on their experience and reality from their own perspective, their efforts have been treated as peripheral or supplementary at best in the growing Third World theologies. To facilitate this needed contribution of Third World women, it is valuable and helpful to examine their experience within a specific Third World theological association.  A serious study of these women's theological journey can assist in determinig which factors can best promote the development of Third World women's theological consciousness.

### The Need for the Study

The need for such a study was made manifest to me in my own experience within the Ecumenical Association of Third World Theologians (EATWOT)[1] and my involvement in working toward a more meaningful theology in the Third World.  My personal involvement in the Association began in January 1976, eight months before its formal establishment. After five years of work, first as staff and then as member and as first woman officer of EATWOT, it became more and more evident that the women's manifest contribution was hardly perceptible. First, there was an unexpressed "macho" ideology in the Association. For example, there was a general assumption within EATWOT that male theologians were more competent and knowledgeable resource persons for its conferences. Secondly, for some time, we ourselves as women members of EATWOT were not clear about the specific contribution we could make precisely as Third World women. With a few exceptions, what we said and wrote reflected a great deal of the male-dominated liberation theology of our own continents. Moreover, the times we EATWOT women incorporated a women's viewpoint in our input, we were largely dependent on First World feminist sources and ideas.

In the course of EATWOT's history, attitudes and practices have changed, as revealed in the chapters that follow. As Third World women theologians we have gradually become conscious that unless the emerging theologies on our continents are inclusive of the women's viewpoint, these theologies cannot be relevant or liberating for ourselves or for the Church or for society at large. However, not only EATWOT women but also our other Third World sisters need help and encouragement so that our theological voice will be authentically ours and will be heard. It is imperative that what we say will not get subsumed but become an integral part of a relevant theology for Third World Christians. It was thus that I decided to make the theological journey of EATWOT women the subject of my doctoral study.[2]

The study attempts to trace the origins and growth of women's theological consciousness within EATWOT and to suggest proper means of promoting this development based on the findings. The approach is primarily descriptive and historical, but one chapter of the study is analytical. As a history, the study uses the third person pronoun required of dissertations in the succeeding chapters, but it makes no claim to objectivity.[3] In the first place, I was, and still am, very much a part of this history. In the second place, as a woman, an Asian, and a Catholic, I can only interpret this history from my own background and vantage point.[4]

### Clarification of Terms

Before proceeding, it is necessary to explain a few terms such as "contextualization of theology," "Third World," and "Third World theologian." As used in this study they need some initial elaboration.

*Contextualization of theology.* The term 'contextualization' was introduced to the theological world in 1972 by the Theological Education Fund (TEF) of the World Council of Churches. Previously, such terms as adaptation, accommodation, inculturation, and indigenization were more commonly used to designate ways of reformulating theology in a context other than the West. In the Third World, there are nuances in the meaning given these terms, but in general they indicate the use of native culture, religion and/or philosophy as the basis of theological reinterpretation. Contextualization does not ignore traditional culture, but goes beyond it in a dynamic way. Thus the TEF speaks of contextualizing theology as taking into account "the process of secularity, technology, and the struggles of human justice"[5] which are part and parcel of Third World reality. The TEF goes on to explain that "contextualization, while it stresses our local and situational concerns, draws its basic power from the Gospel which is for all people."[6]

It is from this original sense that "contextual theology" as used in this study derives its meaning and expands it.[7] Contextualizing theology means, in effect, taking the historical, socio-economic, political, cultural, ethnic, and religious context seriously and using the people's experience within this particular context as the starting point of the theologizing process..

*Third World.* This term has been understood in various ways. It was originally used by the French demographer Alfred Sauvy in 1952, who saw similarity between the nations moving toward independence from colonial powers and the Third Estate in France during the French Revolution.[8] The term soon became an easy and useful designation of the international reality. [9] For EATWOT, however, the term has a supra-geographic sense,[10] describing a social condition characterized by poverty and oppression: massive poverty surrounding small pockets of affluence with an oppressed majority facing a powerful elite.[11] The Third World is marked by economic, political, cultural, racial, gender and/or other forms of oppression; it is the underside of affluence and dominance. Thus for EATWOT, the Third World encompasses even those sections of the so-called First World where groups of people form an oppressed or dominated minority.

For many years, the term has been widely accepted, but recently, its use has been questioned or abandoned.[12] EATWOT, however, retains the use of "Third World" believing that its understanding of the term is still valid.[13]

*Third World theologian.* According to the Association's position, not all theologians living in the Third World are *ipso facto* Third World theologians, just as not all theologies produced in the Third World are Third World theologies. As J. Russell Chandran, first EATWOT president, maintains: "In order to be a Third World theologian one must have an orientation to do theological reflection on the gospel of Jesus Christ as it comes alive in the totality of the struggle of an oppressed people to be fully human."[14] What EATWOT considers Third World theology is necessarily from the vantage point of the poor and oppressed struggling for justice.

Although EATWOT has its own understanding of Third World, in this study the term will have geographic overtones to mean those sectors of Africa, Asia, and Latin America where the quality of life has been diminished by general poverty and exploitation. Thus while my aim is to trace the development of the theological consciousness of women in EATWOT, not all the women members of the Association are included, but only the women from Africa, Asia, and Latin America, with emphasis on the Asian women. EATWOT has women theologians from minority groups in the United States, but because their context is considerably distinct, they are not part of the study. Barring some exceptions, the study further limits itself to the works of the women as found in EATWOT publications, in published or unpublished proceedings of EATWOT consultations, in the women's writings and letters in the EATWOT archives and files, and in the tape recording of personal interviews.

There is an increasing number of publications on Third World theology as well as by Third World theologians. EATWOT members have contributed significantly to this growing pool of material, but there is still relatively little on EATWOT women and their theological contribution or by EATWOT women themselves.[15] The material in these few volumes have also been used as resources for the coming chapters.

## Overview of the Chapters

A brief summary of the contents of the study is helpful at this point. The first chapter begins with an overview of the context of EATWOT's origins as well as factors that led to its foundation in 1976.

The second chapter deals with EATWOT's initial five-year program, and EATWOT women's gradual awareness of their limited role and participation in the program. The chapter also delineates the Association's achievements as well as its limitations as an ecumenical, theological, and liberation-oriented movement during this initial five-year period.

The third chapter focusses on the establishment of the EATWOT Women's Commission in 1983 and its effect on the collective theological consciousness of EATWOT women. Special emphasis is given to the Commission's activities from 1983 to 1986.

The fourth chapter treats the women's activities from their intercontinental conference in 1986 to 1991, noting the similarities and differences between the continents. It includes the results of two consultations designed to deepen and expand the theological thinking of EATWOT women in Asia.

The fifth chapter centers on individual EATWOT women and their theological journeys. The main resources for this chapter are these women's writings besides taped interviews.

The sixth chapter is an analytical overview of commonalities and divergences among Third World women theologians, and factors that have contributed to their theological development.

A brief seventh chapter contains conclusions based on the study, including recommendations regarding the future work that remains to be done within EATWOT and the Women's Commission.

The Afterword is an addition not contained in the original dissertation. It speaks about an important EATWOT event which took place after the study was completed: the 1992 general assembly and its effect on EATWOT women.

## Expectations and Acknowledgements

It is hoped that this study will help in promoting the development of Third World theology from a women's perspective. Without women's contributions, theology in the Third World will be truncated.

It is also hoped that the study will assist those in ministry in the Third World—women and men alike—to recognize and appreciate the input and participation of women. This is imperative if the Church is to become a truly inclusive community, with genuine partnership and cooperation among its members.

A further expectation of this study is that it will promote a better understanding of Third World women, their vision and aspirations, and not only "where they are coming from theologically." Hopefully such an understanding would lead to genuine collegiality among EATWOT men and women, and to greater solidarity not only among Third World women everywhere, but also between First and Third World women in the common task of creating a more just and caring society for all.

I have many hopes and dreams about the future of women's theological work in the Third World, and I wish to remain part of this important effort. Before concluding this introductory section, I wish to acknowledge all those who have helped me along the way. There are those who have contributed useful and insightful suggestions; some have adjusted both work and community schedule to give me the time to write; and others have provided continued support and encouragement. There are a few, however, that I would like to mention specifically: Letty Russell of Yale Divinity School who served as my dissertation advisor; Pui-lan Kwok, presently with the faculty of Episcopal Divinity School in Cambridge, Mass., and Helen R. Graham, MM, of the Institute of Formation and Religious Studies in Quezon City, Philippines, both of whom proofread the dissertation and offered invaluable criticism and suggestions; Eileen Laird and Margaret Lacson, both Maryknoll Sisters, who were most generous with their time and technical assistance; Mary John Mananzan, OSB, of the Institute of Women's Studies in Manila, Philippines, and Sergio Torres of Centro Diego de Medellin in Santiago, Chile, both long-time friends and EATWOT colleagues who were most encouraging and helpful in getting this book published. Last but not least, I want to express my thanks to all the EATWOT women without whose effort and cooperation this book would not be, and to the EATWOT Executive Committee who approved its publication "with enthusiasm." Without doubt, each one who has collaborated in this endeavor shares the conviction that the early attempts of Third World women theologians are a genuine contribution toward the development of inclusive and relevant Third World theologies that should be part of recorded theological history.

# CHAPTER ONE

## A MOVEMENT NAMED EATWOT

> Women are especially discriminated against in the Third World.
> Theology both in the First World and Third World has too long
> been a male, white theology, and should be liberated from these
> constraints . . . The common human experience of women in
> their liberational struggle constitutes a true source of theology.
> Christians must . . . include women's perspectives in their
> theological reflection. Otherwise there can be no truly relevant
> theology . . .(From the final statement of the fifth EATWOT
> conference)[1]

Christian women doing theology in the Third World have slowly
become aware of the truth of this declaration and have grown to
understand their responsibility in creating a Third World theology that
is liberating and life-enhancing for both women and men alike. Not
only Christian communities but society at large stands to benefit from
their effort.

This study centers around a group of Third World women and
how they have come to this realization and have begun to take the
responsibility and challenge seriously. They are women doing theology in Africa, Asia, and Latin America. They are of different races and
of different cultural traditions; they belong to various Christian
denominations and have a variety of theological backgrounds. Their
common denominator is that they are all members of the Ecumenical
Association of Third World Theologians and part of its Women's
Commission. As such they are committed to promoting Third World
theologies that take the women's experience and viewpoint seriously.

To understand these women's distinctive contribution to Third
World theology, it is important first to understand what this emerging

Third World theology is about and what one particular association, EATWOT, has done to promote it. In some way, great or small, these women's theological development and efforts have been affected by this Third World movement called EATWOT.

### The Decade Before EATWOT's Birth

The Ecumenical Association of Third World Theologians, now commonly known as EATWOT, was born in 1976. The decade before its birth (1966-1975) was a period of awakening for the Third World. In the first place, there was the realization that Third World countries share common characteristics. Then, too, there were events in the "global village"—political, economic, socio-cultural and religious— that had marked effects on the peoples of Africa, Asia, and Latin America. A few of these events will be mentioned here, especially those which had bearing on the founding of EATWOT.

Third World countries are the so-called "underdeveloped" or more euphemistically, the "developing" countries.[2] In the economic sphere, though generally rich in natural resources, they are poor in terms of basic goods and facilities. Lacking the proper technology to be self-reliant in utilizing and marketing their resources, they continue to suffer not only from technological dependence but also from uneven trade terms and heavy foreign debt. In the socio-cultural sphere, the majority of the people endure a low standard of living while a powerful elite enjoy an affluent life-style. Although most Third World countries are rich in cultural and religious traditions, there is generally a high rate of illiteracy and unemployment, low standards of health and sanitation, and a high degree of infant mortality. Furthermore, there has been social and economic marginalization of racial groups, women, and members of ethnic and religious minorities, to name some of the major victims of such discrimination.

In the political sphere during the decade prior to EATWOT's founding, there were a growing number of repressive governments, both civilian and military, which had little regard for human and social rights and which were usually backed by foreign powers. Although by the mid-sixties most of the Third World countries had gained their independence, beginning with those in Latin America in the past century, these countries were experiencing a new pattern of domination by their former (or in some cases, newly acquired) colonial masters. Replacing the outmoded formula of direct occupation and colonialization with the "neocolonialism" model, these masters were continuing to direct and control the economic and political life of their former colonies in varying ways and degrees, and were reaping enormous benefits from this uneven relationship.

Neocolonialism came in the form of multinational corporations, unbalanced trade terms, joint "partnerships" with the state, foreign "aid," costly technological "assistance," and so forth. Third World countries were made producers of cash crops, drugs with its destructive effects, and became dumping grounds for inappropriate and outmoded goods from the industrialized countries. The consumerism and tourism that were fostered have been especially damaging to women, many of them forced into becoming "consumer goods" themselves through the commercialization of their own bodies. When and where expedient, authoritarian governments were set up and an ideology of national security promulgated. As this new form of exploitation and domination consolidated itself, the United States emerged as the predominant neocolonial power.

All this was made possible with the acquiescence and collaboration of the local economic and political elite. Many in the Third World were awakening to the fact that they were not so much "underdeveloped" by virtue of limited human and natural resources as they were forced into a state of underdevelopment as a result of years of economic, political, cultural, and even religious dependence.[3] Indeed, the Third World was the "periphery" that had been forced to revolve around and depend on the controlling and powerful "center."

### The Responses to "Underdevelopment"

The issue of the "underdevelopment" of newly independent countries of Africa and Asia was a cause of universal concern. The United Nations (UN) declared the 1960s as a Development Decade (DD1) and the 1970s as the second Development Decade (DD2). The objectives behind these decades are clearly seen in the preamble to DD2: "to create conditions of stability and well-being and to ensure a minimum standard of living consistent with human dignity through economic and social progress and development." [4] Thus the member nations of the UN were to pledge themselves to pursue policies that would "create a more rational world order in which equality of opportunity should be as much a prerogative of nations as of individuals within a nation."[5] However, by the middle of DD2, it was becoming evident that, as in DD1, action did not match the words of the Preamble; the decades failed to narrow the breach between "developed" and "underdeveloped." This failure was further aggravated by conflicts between Third World countries themselves.

It is not surprising that the period from the mid-sixties to the mid-seventies was also a period of social unrest, protest, and revolt. There was a rise in people's movements to make their demands heard, but the response of the powers-that-be was usually one of repression, which was generally backed by foreign powers. In many Third World countries, national liberation movements were active, some succeeding in replacing the dominant capitalistic system with a more self-reliant socialist development.[6]

There were events that brought a ray of hope to Third World peoples. The first was the meetings of the UN Conference of Trade and Development (UNCTAD).[7] This was part of a continuing attempt of Third World leaders to obtain better prices for their exports, ensure integrated commodity agreements, reschedule their external debt, limit or control the multinational corporations and military bases, and regulate the transfer of technology.[8]

A second event was the successful attempt in 1973 of the Organization of Petroleum Exporting Countries (OPEC), mostly of the Middle East, in setting the price of oil and securing for themselves an enormous amount of "petrol dollars." Although the poor, oil-importing Third World countries were hurt financially by this OPEC move, they saw what was possible when Third World countries band together to take a common stand vis-a-vis powerful industrialized nations of the First World.[9]

A third event was the proposal for a New International Economic Order (NIEO) adopted by UN sessions in 1974 and 1975. In those years there were clear indications that the current economic order was in conflict with the just aspirations of Third World nations and that the crisis in the world economy had severe repercussions principally on those nations. A special session in 1974 approved a declaration asking for the establishment of an NIEO based on equity, interdependence, and the common interest and cooperation of all the nations.[10]

The question of social and economic development was not ignored by those who exercised Christian leadership during this decade prior to EATWOT's founding. In the Catholic world, this was the period immediately after the Second Vatican Council (1962-

1965).[11]  Although as an ecumenical council, Vatican II was still highly Western in its outlook, it had a global impact and introduced the "most profound wave of change to sweep the Church since the Reformation."[12]  The first post-Vatican decade (1966-1976) saw the publication of internationally acclaimed Church documents, such as the encyclical, "On the Development of Peoples," written by Pope Paul VI in 1967, and "Justice in the World," issued by the Synod of Catholic Bishops in 1971. Prompted by Vatican II, but going beyond it, these documents set the social question in a worldwide context. Paul VI's encyclical stressed the right to self-development and national self-determination on the part of the world's poor, proclaiming development as the new name for peace. The bishops' document identified the struggle for justice and peace as a central element in the Church's renewal, suggesting that the Church must stand with the poor and oppressed if it is to be faithful to the Gospel mandate.

On the Protestant side, the World Council of Churches (WCC) held two Assemblies within this period: in Uppsala in 1968 and in Nairobi in 1975.  "Behold I make all things new" was Uppsala's theme, which challenged the churches to listen to the cries of the world and to anticipate God's reign in joyful worship and daring acts. The report of the Assembly in Uppsala showed a shift from attention to "freedom" and "order" to concern for "social justice" and "human dignity." The Programme to Combat Racism was one of the fruits of this Assembly. The WCC Assembly in Nairobi moved still further, taking up the issues of peace and disarmament, and human rights.  It was also the first time a WCC Assembly dealt with sexism, a year after the first world conference for women which WCC organized in Berlin in 1974 with the title, "Sexism in the 1970s—Discrimination Against Women."[13]

At this time, Third World churches themselves started to make their own impact on the world, announcing their "coming of age."  In Latin America, at the second general meeting of the Latin American Episcopal Conference (CELAM) in 1968, the Catholic bishops issued what became more widely known as the Medellin documents, declaring that the Church should take an option for the poor. The documents' forceful social criticism and prophetic commitment reverberated around the world.  Based on a critical analysis of Latin American society and its unjust economic and political structures, the documents called for conscientization and both personal and societal transformation in order to achieve genuine peace and liberation.[14]  The influence of the emerging Latin American theology of liberation is evident in the documents.

In Africa in 1974, the Third Assembly of the All African Conference of Churches (AACC) dared the young churches to begin a "moratorium" on overseas aid in personnel and material resources, in order to end their crippling dependency on the "older churches" and to become self-reliant ecclesial communities. The AACC bid drew immediate reactions, both negative and positive, from all over the Christian world.[15] A year earlier, in 1973, the East Asian Christian Conference broadened its ecumenical network and became the Christian Conference of Asia (CCA).

In the theological arena, liberation theology had begun to create an impact on the Third World, notably with the publication and translation of Gustavo Gutierrez's *A Theology of Liberation*.[16] James Cone's *Black Theology and Black Power*[17] published in the United States in 1970 had a special influence on young black pastors and theologians in South Africa. Still another important form of liberation theology was in its initial stages in the West—feminist theology—but it was still little known or appreciated in most of the Third World at this time.

This period of challenge and growth in liberal and even progressive ideas was also a period of reaction and counter movements in the churches. On the Protestant side, at the World Congress on Evangelism held in Berlin in 1966, the Evangelical Christians openly voiced their opposition to what they saw as theological compromise and syncretistic concessions made by the WCC. On the Catholic side, while the pronouncements of Pope Paul VI and local Churches showed progressive tendencies, the trend within the Vatican bureaucracy was to preserve the status quo. The Apostolic Nuncios especially often maintained a friendly attitude toward repressive regimes that overtly or covertly opposed the Church in their respective countries. In Latin America in 1972, four years after Medellin, when Bishop Alfonso Lopez Trujillo was elected general secretary of CELAM, there began a "systematic persecution of liberation theology and of Christians who try to make a more scientific analysis of reality."[18]

### The Roots of EATWOT

It was thus in an awakening Third World that EATWOT was born in 1976. But this birthing process was a slow one. The idea of an organized dialogue among Third World theologians was first conceived two years earlier in the intuition of an African theological student at the Catholic University of Louvain in Belgium. Oscar K. Bimwenyi of Zaire remembers how he had been invited to India for a trip of several weeks and how he could not help noting the many similarities between the socio-economic, political, and religious situations in India and those in his native Africa. He became concerned that while organizations existed in the socioeconomic sphere to foster understanding among the so-called "underdeveloped" countries so they could work together toward a better world, oddly enough, there was nothing comparable in the field of theology. Upon his return to Louvain, he shared his report and vision with friends.[19] Together they moved towards translating Bimwenyi's vision of a tricontinental colloquium into reality.

The first step was to form an organizing committee made up of theology students from different Third World countries, with a coordinator for each continent.[20] The second step was to send letters to thirty theologians on the three continents to ask their opinions on the projected colloquium.[21] Bimwenyi recalls: "The idea of a tricontinental meeting of Asian, African, and Latin American theologians met with a warm and often enthusiastic reception everywhere. It evidently came as an answer to something people had long been waiting for."[22] Indeed, as the Third World was awakening, Christians themselves, as individuals and in basic communities, were being challenged to rethink and renew. Responses confirmed that the time was ripe for new and bold initiatives.[23]

The initial steps led to the implementation stage. A meeting was set for November 1975 in Louvain to discuss the organization of the projected dialogue and another meeting was set for the following month in Nairobi to finalize the coordination.[24] The fifth general assembly of the WCC in Nairobi provided a convenient setting for this second meeting as theologians from Africa, Asia, and Latin America were expected to be there. Together with these theologians, the organizers agreed to form a steering committee for the dialogue.[25]

The organizers agreed to call the tricontinental meeting the Ecumenical Dialogue of Third World Theologians.[26] Sometimes the prefix "first" was used, ostensibly with the hope that other dialogues would follow. Though there had been previous Church-related conferences with Third World theologians as participants, the Dialogue was indeed a "first" in several ways. It was the first meeting of its kind planned independently and ecumenically, where Roman Catholics and Protestants were equal partners in a theological venture, without the domination of any ecclesiastical power. Thus from the start, "ecumenical" took on a broad meaning to indicate the participation of both Roman Catholics and Protestants.

It was also the first time theologians from the continents of Asia, Africa, and Latin America held a tri-continental meeting on an equal basis.[27] Moreover, for the first time it could be claimed that the dialogue was truly *of* Third World theologians where the agenda was really their own. It was the first theological event where the "periphery" chose its agenda without involving the "center" and became the focal point of its own theology.[28] In previous Church-related global meetings to which Third World theologians had been invited, not only was the agenda set by the "center"; the meetings involved the active participation of people from the "center." [29] Among such meetings was Theology in the Americas (TIA), held in Detroit in 1975, which provided for exchange between those looking for an alternative to the dominant white, male theology of the United States and liberation theologians from Latin America.[30]

At the planning meeting in Nairobi, the organizers agreed to hold the tricontinental meeting at the Tabora Seminary in Kipalapala, Tanzania, in August of 1976.[31] The general plans completed, Sergio Torres, acting as executive secretary of the steering committee, thereupon flew to Tanzania where he met with President Julius Nyerere who promised his support and participation in the Dialogue. After Torres made the other necessary contacts and arrangements, he returned to New York, where as executive secretary of TIA he had an office and staff, and embarked on the implementation of the plans for the Dialogue.[32]

The proposed program consisted of three parts: "(1) socio-political and cultural analysis of the background of each continent, (2) an evaluation of the presence of the Church on the three continents, and (3) efforts toward a theological approach in the Third World."[33] Twenty-two theologians were invited: seven from Africa, seven from Asia, seven from Latin America and the Caribbean, and one from the black minority in the United States.[34] One lone woman was invited: Beatriz Melano Couch from Argentina.[35] Each participant was asked to prepare a paper representing one aspect of the theological effort in his or her own continent. Couch was requested to write on "New Trends in Latin American Protestant Theology."[36]

The time finally came for the Dialogue. At the last minute the venue was changed, and participants found themselves being ushered from the airport to the campus of the University of Dar es Salaam instead of to the seminary in Kipalapala. The building assigned to them was still under construction. Nevertheless, from August 5 to 12, 1976, while electricians and plumbers scurried about to put on the finishing touches, the twenty-two Third World theologians held their theological deliberations aimed at scrutinizing the "signs of the times," listening to the Spirit amid the division between the rich and the poor, and distinguishing between the dominant and the emerging perspectives operating in the theological world.

Torres recalls that historic meeting as follows:

> Without fully realizing the significance of this meeting, the group accomplished their aim and responded to the Spirit's inspiration. In a few days they were able to know one another, to listen to and learn from one another, and to try to learn about the different cultures and histories of each. They experienced joy, emotion and Utopian dreams. But there were also moments of tension, disillusionment, and confrontation . . .37

### The Beginnings of EATWOT

The Dialogue was not an easy process. The participants were theologians who not only came from four continents and met one another for the first time, but who also represented three Christian traditions: Catholic, Protestant and Orthodox. Furthermore, they were from various races and cultures, speaking three different languages. Besides the varied contexts of the participants, there was also an obvious variety of theological orientations, so it was difficult to come to mutual understanding. Some theologians obviously had a liberational thrust, while others seemed to favor a theology of development or some form of theological adaptation. The Asians and Africans, while recognizing the contribution and creativity of the Latin American theologians, had a cautious attitude toward their liberation theology, considering it still too Western and fearing the possibility of its becoming a new form of dominant theology in the Third World.38

Despite these difficulties and differences, the group in Dar es Salaam realized they shared many similarities and came to a remarkable degree of unity. They agreed that the theology they had inherited from the West was clearly inadequate for responding to the realities and concerns of their regions, and that a new theological model was necessary which would be more relevant to their Third World context. All this is reflected in the final statement. In the end, the theologians could say that the Dar Dialogue was for them "a unique experience of theologizing from, as it were, the other side of the earth and of human history."[39]

At the close of the conference, the participants saw the need for ongoing dialogue and exchange.[40] Thus, though there were differences in theological orientation, they resolved to carry on their fellowship in the form of an association. As stated in the Dar communique, "they found this experience and the consensus in their discussion so worthwhile that they decided that more ecumenical gatherings of Third World theologians would be highly desirable for promoting the doing of theology in the context of Third World social, political, economic, religious, and cultural realities." [41]

Thus was born the Ecumenical Association of Third World Theologians in Dar es Salaam on August 12, 1976.[42] Adopting a provisional constitution, the founding members defined the Association's aim as "the continuing development of Third World Christian theologies which will serve the church's mission in the world and witness to the new humanity in Christ expressed in the struggle for a just society." [43] The Association chose for its officers J. Russell Chandran of India as president, Patrick A. Kalilombe of Malawi as vice president, with Sergio Torres of Chile as executive secretary.

The communique circulated after the establishment of EATWOT lists its four objectives: "(1) sharing with one another the present trends in interpretation of the Gospel in different Third World countries, particularly bearing in mind the role of theology in relation to other faiths and ideologies as well as in relation to the struggle for a just society; (2) promoting the exchange of theological views through writings in books and periodicals of Third World countries; (3) promoting mutual interaction between theological formulation and social analysis; and (4) keeping close contacts with as well as being involved in action-oriented movements for social change."[44]

The stated objectives of the Association actually reflect the main features of the theological model that was agreed on in Dar es Salaam and which EATWOT has hoped to develop and promote. The first is a serious analysis and understanding of one's realities as part of the theologizing process. The group in Dar agreed that without a proper comprehension of their socio-economic, political, and cultural realities, theologians could not interpret God's will in a meaningful way for societies in the Third World.

The second feature of the EATWOT theological model is a new methodological approach that places commitment and involvement as the prior act of theology. Theological reflection comes afterwards. Such an approach is a reversal of the conventional way of theologizing, which begins with concepts and principles and relies heavily on theories and academic research.[45] The Dar group pronounced as irrelevant the academic type of theology produced in libraries and universities that is divorced from action affecting people's lives and struggles.[46]

Thus from the start, EATWOT's theological approach has been contextual, liberational, and ecumenical. Also from the start, EATWOT has realized it does not have a monopoly on this methodological approach. Its concern is to contribute to the collective effort to reformulate theology so as to make it more attuned to, and expressive of, the real aspirations of the struggling peoples of the Third World.

### The Dar Experience Assessed

The Dar es Salaam dialogue created a stir in theological circles in both the Third and First Worlds. For some, it was more than a meeting; it was an event and a symbol. As an event, it marked the beginning of a new era in the history of theology. To quote EATWOT's first executive secretary: "For a moment, (theological) history seemed to have stopped—effectively, to have changed direction."[47] Those who were theologically `voiceless' were now being heard as they openly critiqued the old way and proposed a new way of doing theology. The former learners and consumers of Western theology were now dramatically challenging what they had received from their European and North American mentors and providers.

Moreover, it was a concerted voice that the "center" now heard from the "periphery." The Dar event allowed Third World theologians to share their critiques and to create together. As James Cone, black theologian and EATWOT member, put it:

> Although many theologians of Africa, Asia and Latin America had already begun to offer challenging critiques of the dominant theology . . . they were not keenly aware of each other's critiques

> . . . and were even less knowledgeable of the creative theological alternatives that each was seeking to provide. Third World theologians were developing critiques and constructing theological projects in isolation, as if they had nothing to learn from each other . . . The formation of EATWOT at the 1976 Tanzania meeting represents an attempt of Third World theologians to bring to an end their destructive isolation.[48]

It was with good reason that the respected European theologian, Marie-Dominique Chenu, referred to the Dar event as "the Bandung of theology."[49] A new irreversible stage in theology has begun and Dar es Salaam has become its symbolic starting point.

The Third World theologians who gathered for the Dialogue admitted the frustration they had felt for some time over the "universal theology" that had been imposed upon them. They realized that the so-called "universal theology" they had received was in fact a European-centered interpretation of the Christian faith and actually a form of cultural domination. In their own settings and within their own local communities, many of them had already begun to explore an alternative theological discourse, an interpretation of God's will on the basis of their local conditions and their lived experience of suffering and struggle as Third World peoples.

The displacement of theology from the "center" to the "periphery" was not, however, only geographical or cultural; it was first and foremost epistemological. As recorded in their final statement, the Third World theologians, while affirming their faith in Jesus Christ, announced their preparedness for "a radical break in epistemology which makes commitment the first act of theology and engages in critical reflection on the praxis of the reality of the Third World."[50] Thus, to arrive at truth is not a matter of conforming one's mind to the given in Western philosophical tradition, but of being involved in the process of transforming this world into one that is more just and human. Though perhaps not all who gathered in Dar were aware of the implications of this assertion, nonetheless, it has been subsequently acknowledged that this epistemological break constitutes "the most novel aspect of the Third World theologies and that which differentiates them from traditional academic theology . . . This agreement on the primacy of praxis was one of the fundamental points at Dar es Salaam."[51]

The Dar group recognized that all forms of oppression are "interrelated and interwoven in a complex system of domination;"[52]

however, they spoke more at length of imperialistic and political domination and only cursorily about racism and sexism. While the final statement admitted that "women have been discriminated against and oppressed on all levels of both society and the church,"[53] in none of the post-conference assessment was there an allusion to Couch's token presence at Dar.

Though there were significant agreements, the group in Dar did not reach a consensus on *one* specific Third World theology. But the final mood of the dialogue did not preclude such a consensus as a future possibility. Despite differing opinions in the course of the dialogue, in the end the need for unity and reconciliation was evident. If they were to respond responsibly as Third World citizens and Christians to the reality of poverty, misery, and marginalization in their respective continents, as well as to remain true to the goals and objectives of their new association, it was vital that the theological process they began in Dar should continue.

# CHAPTER TWO
◆ ◆ ◆

## EATWOT'S FIRST FIVE YEARS

Before leaving Dar es Salaam, the members of the newly-formed association planned a five-year program of conferences and agreed to hold their next meeting in Accra, Ghana, the following year. They foresaw a series of inter-continental conferences as the main means of implementing the objectives of the Association.[1] Each conference would focus on a particular Third World continent to understand its realities and challenges as well as to determine the response of the Churches and theology in the region.

### EATWOT'S Initial Five-year Program

From 1976 to 1981, EATWOT held four more conferences. The second EATWOT dialogue planned for Accra, Ghana, was held from December 17 to 23, 1977. The third took place in Wennappuwa, Sri Lanka, from January 7 to 20, 1979. The fourth was in Sao Paulo, Brazil, from February 20 to March 2, 1980, and the fifth, which was to synthesize the findings of the previous conferences, took place in New Delhi, India, from August 17 to 29, 1981. In each of these subsequent dialogues, there was an organizing committee made up of members from the region. Theologians from the other EATWOT regions as well as guests were invited to attend. A panoramic view of each of the subsequent dialogues reveals that the women's recognition of the need for women's liberation within EATWOT itself was a slow and gradual process.

The three conferences after Dar followed the general schema of the initial ecumenical dialogue while focusing on the reality of the particular continent, and took as basic assumptions some of the conclusions of the first dialogue. Besides the new epistemological approach, there were other common understandings that flowed from the Dar discussions and final statement. These were to be taken into consideration in the continuing effort to reformulate theology according to the reality of the Third World.

*God as a God of the poor.* Any Third World theology must be relevant to the poor, who are the majority in Third World continents, and to those oppressed in terms of race, sex, and/or social class.

*Faith as praxis-based.* For the Third World, the "*faith* that seeks understanding" is one that goes beyond mere intellectual acceptance of the biblical message to an authentic following of Jesus. Therefore, Third World theology is meaningful only when it is based on a committed faith in the service of the poor and oppressed. Social analysis becomes a useful interpretative tool to engage in transformative action in favor of the victims of domination.

*A new reading of Scripture.* Scripture remains basic to Third World theology, but it can no longer be interpreted along confessional lines or based on old doctrinal norms that have been a source of division among the Christian churches. Rather Scripture must be seen as "grace" or "judgment" from the perspective of the poor of the world, to which Scripture rightly belongs. This calls forth a new *ecumenism* in theology that cuts across ecclesiastical boundaries at the service of the poor.

These basic criteria for the reformulation of theology in the Third World were presented in the EATWOT executive secretary's opening address at the Accra conference, as he reminded the participants of the task that lay before them.[2]

The theme chosen by the organizing committee of the Accra conference was "The Christian Commitment in Africa Today: Concerns of Emerging Christian Theologies," but the conference was more commonly referred to as the Pan-African Conference of Third World Theologians. Of the ninety participants, there were seventy-three men and seventeen women.[3] Twenty African countries were represented. The final communique summarizes the salient points covered in the deliberations: the present African reality and its historical roots, the presence of Christianity in Africa as missionary Church and as emerging local communities, and the trends in African theology, their sources, characteristics, and perspective for the future.

The conference papers and discussions showed three major

theological trends: theologies of adaptation, critical types of African theologies, and the South African Black theology of liberation. Proponents of each trend were present at the conference. The discussions also showed a wide variety of sources for the emerging Christian theologies. Besides the Bible and Christian tradition, other rich founts surfaced: African life and cultural heritage, African anthropology and cosmology, African traditional religions and the newly established Independent churches, and the African experience of struggle against all forms of oppression. Though Mercy Oduyoye's paper rued the "limitation placed on women's participation in religious practices"[4] the situation of women was discussed but minimally and the other women's papers dealt mostly with women's church-related roles in present-day Africa.[5]

EATWOT's third intercontinental dialogue held in Sri Lanka was also known as the Asian Theological Conference (ATC).[6] Its title, "Asia's Struggle for Full Humanity: Towards a Relevant Theology," represented both its theme and its task. A novel part of the conference was the three-day exposure program required of the eighty participants. Its purpose was to deepen the participants' understanding of the complex Asian reality and to help them surface pressing theological issues. The sixty-two men and eighteen women—professional theologians, social activists, church workers, students, educators, bishops, religious sisters, priests, and ministers—each chose a "live-in" experience among villagers or fisherfolk, tea or coconut plantation workers, industrial workers, trade union personnel, women in special training projects, youth and students in collective farms, or minority groups and slumdwellers.

This inductive approach clearly demonstrated how one's interpretation of reality very much conditions the direction of one's theology. This was further reinforced by Marianne Katoppo's presentation of Asian theology from an Asian woman's perspective, her reflections based on her experience as a Minahasa woman in Indonesia and on women's reality in Asia.[7] Unfortunately, her paper, though appreciated, was overshadowed by the tension that arose over the differing readings of the live-in experiences[8] as well as of the Asian context itself.

One of the other resource persons, Aloysius Pieris of Sri Lanka, characterized Asia's overwhelming poverty and its multifaceted religiosity as two realities which "in their interpenetration constitute what might be designated as the Asian context and which is the matrix of any theology that is truly Asian."[9]   He presented poverty as the common denominator between Asia and the rest of the Third World, and religiosity as giving the continent its specific Asian character. Polarized positions ensued over this characterization, some claiming the priority of Asia's "Third-worldness" over its "Asian-ness" in the search for a relevant theology, since it is the poverty and oppression that have hindered Asian peoples in their search for full humanity. Others insisted on the religio-cultural rather than the socio-economic as the main base of a truly Asian theology.[10]

Tensions and shortcomings notwithstanding, the participants agreed that the conference was an experience to be shared and they decided to write a final statement. The statement describes the Asian context and the main theological issues, the work towards a new theology and spirituality that will speak to Asian peoples, and future tasks that include new directions in formation programs, and the building of networks and alliances with those similarly engaged in the struggle for full humanity.

For the first time in an EATWOT statement, the domination and multiple oppression of Asian women was seen as a theological issue to be dealt with, but there was little discussion of it in the actual conference. The statement admitted the limited scope allowed women in the process of economic production at all levels as well as their sexual and intellectual vulnerability in Asian societies. "An interaction of traditional and modern forces (especially tourism) compels them to compromise with consumeristic values of capitalistic society."[11]  Again these thoughts were not discussed, nor was it considered whether or not these had any implications for EATWOT in Asia.

EATWOT's fourth intercontinental conference held in Sao Paulo in 1980 carried the name "International Ecumenical Congress of Theology." The Latin American organizing committee chose as conference theme, "The Ecclesiology of Basic Christian Communities."[12]  Having worked on their theology of liberation for over a decade, the Latin American theologians felt it was time to focus on the ecclesial aspects of the large, and still growing, number of small grass roots Christian communities, whose faith and life struggles form the roots of liberation theology. It was not to be an academic discussion but mainly an interchange concerning the communities' experience as church from the perspective of the Church's preferential option for the poor. The interest in such an exchange was obvious; it was the biggest of the EATWOT conferences, the participants coming from forty-two countries and numbering 180 in all. But of the total number, less than one fifth were women.

The conference recognized the contribution of the Christian communities in terms of their participation in popular social movements as well as their stirring witness as victims of persecution and repression and even as martyrs in their attempt to follow Jesus. The conference, however, was not limited to theological reflection on popular Christian communities. It also included an analysis of the structures of domination, but only in a cursory manner as to how these have oppressed Latin American women, blacks, and indigenous peoples. The final statement challenged the Church to recover its primordial "spirituality of liberation," invited it to be converted from its personal and structural sins, and pleaded for "greater intercommunication and mutual help, with greater effectiveness and ecumenical spirit, within the liberating process of the churches of the Third World."[13]

While the final statement declared the discrimination against women in church ministries as biblically, theologically, and pastorally unjustifiable,[14] the conference itself was still clearly male-oriented and male-dominated. There was an effort to have women give reports and personal testimonies,[15] but they were greatly outnumbered by the male presenters of social analysis, biblical and theological discourse, and personal experience.

The last theological dialogue in EATWOT's initial five-year program was held in New Delhi in 1981 on the occasion of EATWOT's first general assembly. It was to be a synthesis conference that would, at the same time, determine EATWOT's future direction. Though often referred to as EATWOT V, the conference was appropriately entitled "Irruption of the Third World,"[16] for EATWOT, as a new movement of theologians for justice, was indeed a concrete manifestation of the irrupting Third World. In addition, the conference was fittingly located in Asia where three fourths of the Third World lives.

### The Delhi Experience

The task of the fifty delegates and observers who gathered in Delhi was to examine both the commonalities and uniqueness of the continental efforts to contextualize theology as well as to delve into the significance of EATWOT as a movement not only in the Third

World but in relation to the established theology as well. This, in effect, would synthesize EATWOT's effort of the past five years. Because this culminating work was at the same time a general assembly, an equal number of delegates from the three Third World regions, together with representatives from U.S. minorities and the Caribbean, were present for this event. There were but ten women among the total of forty-two EATWOT delegates in Delhi.

EATWOT V was preceded by a year of collective study and reflection in each region as preparation for the conference. Local meetings were held to examine the socio-economic and political situation in the region, the prevailing worldviews, the involvement of the local churches, and current efforts towards inculturation or contextualization of theology. To facilitate further the task of EATWOT V, the conference organizers designed an exposure to the Indian reality reflective of the Third World, allowed time for intra-continental sharing to produce consolidated reports, and invited resource persons to speak on three key topics: the existing global systems and structures, the significant role of culture and other religions in Third World theology, and biblical hermeneutics from the viewpoint of the oppressed.

Pieris' talk on "The Place of Non-Christian Religions and Cultures in the Evolution of Third World Theology"[17] created an impact on the conference, for he brought home the hitherto overlooked point that "the irruption of the Third World is also the irruption of the non-Christian world. The vast majority of God's poor perceive their ultimate concern and symbolize their struggle for liberation in the idiom of non-Christian religions and cultures."[18] Pieris' assertion carries far-reaching implications not only for theological renewal but for societal transformation as well, the twin tasks the Third World theologians have chosen for themselves. To be effective and relevant, Third World theology needs to take the experience and aspirations of the "non-Christian" majority seriously. Even theologians from the predominantly Christian countries of Latin America and the Philippines saw they were not exempt from this exigency.

In the discussions that followed the reports and input, commonalities and differences started to emerge, but not without heat, and even resentment. It was difficult to discuss theological issues through an interpreter but it was even more frustrating to understand terms in varying ways depending on one's context and experience. One such term was "poverty."

To the majority of Third World theologians in Delhi, poverty meant material deprivation. For the Latin Americans, it is larely an evil to be eliminated, while for the Asians, it is both a sin and a virtue—a sin when it is imposed from the outside; a virtue when it is voluntarily embraced. For the Asian Buddhist monk, for example, voluntary poverty is both salutary and liberating, for it frees him from greed and overattachment to possessions.[19] For the African theologians, however, poverty had an anthropological significance. Engelbert Mveng poignantly expressed it: "There is a type of poverty that I call 'anthropological poverty.' It consists in despoiling human beings not only of what they have but of everything that constitutes their being and essence—their identity, history, ethnic roots, language, culture, faith, creativity, dignity, pride, ambitions, right to speak . . ."[20]

It soon became obvious that it was premature to speak of a synthesis of the past five years, or to claim that there was but *one* Third World theology. There were too many points that needed clarification and further discussion. The disagreements that surfaced were rooted, strangely enough, not on confessional affiliation, but rather on theological approach, or on political orientation, or, for the first time in an EATWOT conference, on gender difference.

### "The Irruption within the Irruption"

In the ensuing confrontation, it became apparent to EATWOT women that their theological contribution was being taken only lightly and even rejected by some of the EATWOT men. But even before the conference, the women already felt slighted when no woman was chosen as resource person for the conference. Also at the time, all three EATWOT officers were men. It dawned upon the women that despite the supportive statements regarding women's equality and the declarations against sexism in all the past conference documents, the reality was different. Both disturbed and disappointed, the EATWOT women decided it was time to demand their rightful place not only in society but in the association as well. Oduyoye referred to this as the "irruption within the irruption" in her assessment of the Delhi event.[21]

The "irruption" had an obvious effect on the final document of the Delhi conference, which contained more references to women than any of the previous conference statements. The statement was explicit in admitting that "irruption of the Third World" also meant "women demanding recognition and equality" (par. 26). Besides the usual allusions to sexism, the statement acknowledged, for instance, that women have contributed to the development of Third World countries and yet are still only accorded "minority" status (par. 17) Treated as inferior, they suffer inequality in job opportunities and remuneration. The statement also confessed that "all religions without exception are discriminating against women" (par. 17). If Christian theology and the church sincerely believe that all humanity, both male and female, are created in God's image, then they must do more than simply make room for women in ecclesiastical disciplines and institutions that remain patriarchal at heart (par. 49). In its concluding section, the Delhi statement pronounced as one of EATWOT's priorities for the next five-year period, "supporting women's struggle for equality in and through theology" (par.73).[22]

While recognizing that all this was tantamount to an "act of contrition" on the part of the EATWOT men and was a move in the right direction, the EATWOT women felt that the Association had to do more than make challenging statements about women's inequality and oppression. The more significant outcome of the "irruption" will be detailed in the next chapter.

The last day of the Delhi meeting was devoted to the business of the general assembly. The Constitution was revised to contain a new administrative structure and to include the creation of working commissions; seven new officers were elected which included a woman for the first time;[23] and a fresh direction for EATWOT was given for the next five years. It was agreed that for the period 1981-1986, the concentration of EATWOT's work should be, but not exclusively, on the regional rather than on the inter-continental level. It was clear that if Third World theology is truly contextual, the uniqueness of each region should first be allowed to emerge before a common Third World theology could come to be. Thus, despite the shortcomings and differences and a lack of explicit guidelines, it was unanimously decided that the work of EATWOT should continue for at least another five years.

### EATWOT's Achievements

What has EATWOT accomplished in its first five years? Even as the Delhi Conference was going on, EATWOT members asked themselves this question. Several task forces had been set up during the conference to prepare for the assembly, and among them was the "Future of EATWOT" task force, which assessed EATWOT's past in order to propose its direction for the coming years.

*Accomplishments.* The evaluation of the "Future of EATWOT" task force showed the following positive aspects:

EATWOT has contributed to the development of contextual theologies in different regions of the Third World. It has provided an independent forum for dialogue, challenge, and mutual enrichment among Third World theologians, and has been able to create a basis for an understanding of a Third World theology that respects both the common realities of Third World countries and the particularities of each region. In addtion, EATWOT's bulletin *(Voices from the Third World)*, documents, and books have been an important service to people involved in theological education and to those in contact with grass roots organizations. Through EATWOT's efforts, there has been a change of attitude towards Third World theologies among First World theologians.[24]

The task force evaluation also indicated shortcomings. Among those mentioned were: (1) the academic style of the EATWOT conferences has inhibited the participation of the poor and oppressed; (2) the centralized form of the Association's administration has resulted in the passivity of many members; and (3) EATWOT was too dependent on First World funding.[25]

*Methodology.* Although in Delhi, there was no common agreement on a Third World theology that everyone could support, the final statement pointed to elements of a common methodology for Third World theologies.

1. The starting point for Third World theologies is the struggle of the poor and the oppressed against all forms of injustice and domination. Thus the experience of the Third World is a veritable source of theology.

2. The poor and oppressed have the right to reflect on their own lives and their own faith in God.

3. The faith-based life interpretations of the people, expressed in their cultural idioms, liturgy, songs and poetry, constitute genuine theology.

4. The Bible, as an integral basis of faith reflection, needs to be reread in light of the hermeneutical privilege of the poor, that is, from the perspective of the underside of history.

5. Both committed action and silent contemplation are neces-

sary for genuine theological reflection.

6. Social analysis is a basic tool for a liberating theology in order to interpret God's will for our societies.

7. A relevant theology for the Third World should take seriously both the religio-cultural and the socio-economic aspects of the people's lives. Just as necessary as social analysis is the identification of the liberating aspects of religions and cultures on the one hand, and their alienating, domesticating features on the other. [26]

*EATWOT's theological assumptions and convictions.* In Delhi, it was obvious that each continent had its particular emphasis: Africa's accent was on culture and indigenization; Latin America's, on social analysis and socioeconomic transformation; Asia's, on religious and cultural plurality. Nevertheless, the final statement of the conference manifested common theological assumptions and convictions, among which are the following:

1. The struggle for a just world and full humanity constitutes participation in God's creative plan.

2. Poverty as experienced by the majority in the world is a degradation of the divine image on earth and a diminution of human dignity and personhood.

3. God rejects oppression and every form of injustice whether on the basis of race, sex, class, or creed.

4. The sacred scriptures and traditions of other faiths are also a source of revelation for us.

5. Life can be more human and in keeping with biblical revelation through a more egalitarian and communitarian reorganization of our societies.

6. Discipleship calls for the transformation of social structures and the renewal of cultures as well as a conversion of ourselves and of our distorted relationships.

7. Just as the experience of the Third World as a true source of theology must be taken seriously, *so also must the common human experience of women in their liberational struggle be taken seriously* (emphasis mine). [27]

Though these theological assumptions and convictions were accepted in principle by the participants in the Delhi conference, how deeply they were held by the individual theologian was something else. [28] In like manner, though no one contested the "Future of EATWOT" evaluation of the Association's performance in its first stage, to what degree the individual members agreed with the listing is again another matter. The EATWOT women themselves would have listed one additional shortcoming: the marginal role of the female members in the life of the Association.

While this was not articulated as such at the assembly, Oduyoye spoke for most EATWOT women when she wrote her reflections on the Delhi experience: "EATWOT had come face to face with the fact that the community of women and men, even in the church and among `liberation theologians,' is not as liberating as it could be." [29] This was particularly obvious at the assembly session when some male members stood to object to Jacqueline Grant's use of "Mother/Father God" in a worship session, deriding it as both untheological and unbiblical. It was even taken as a joke by some when Katoppo called the attention of the session to the need to watch "our language about God and before God." However, it was no comic relief; rather it signaled the irruption within the irruption, trumpeting the existence of some other hurts, spotlighting women's marginalization from the theological enterprise and indeed from decision-making in the churches . . . That 'irruption' could only have come from a woman. But why at New Delhi and not before? The answer is simple; the process of involving women in meaningful roles in EATWOT did not begin at the initial stages.[30]

The Delhi meeting ended with many challenges that demanded a response. To EATWOT women, the "irruption within the irruption" was one of them. To them, it signified both a protest and a demand. Without many words, the women made it known that they no longer wanted to be token presences or fill quotas at EATWOT meetings, or just be politely listened to and then ignored. EATWOT structures and practices would henceforth have to reflect the unity and equality in Christ that Christians claim. EATWOT agendas would need to address sexism-in-community as a theological issue if indeed the Association seeks a truly just world.

For EATWOT women, the "irruption" also signaled awareness; a deepening for some, a beginning for others. It forged a stronger sense of bondedness not only among the women but with their struggling sisters the world over. In the end, the "irruption" in Delhi was but a microcosm of the greater irruption of Third World women beginning to occur in both church and society. It was but part of "the voice of the earth's voiceless beginning to penetrate the atmosphere and disturb the peace of the principalities and powers that hold the structures of our world in their hands."[31]

# CHAPTER THREE
◆ ◆ ◆

## THE EATWOT WOMEN'S COMMISSION

### The Setting

The "irruption within the irruption" in the Delhi event took place in 1981. It was not until two years later that the women took concrete steps to have their theological voices heard and their full participation ensured in EATWOT. The occasion was the Sixth International Conference of the Association, more popularly known as the Dialogue between First and Third World Theologians.[1] The setting was Geneva, Switzerland; the time, January 5 to 13, 1983. The total of eighty participants from both the First and Third Worlds included ten women from Third World countries: two from Africa, five from Asia, and three from Latin America.[2] The dialogue turned out to have a marked effect on these EATWOT women.

Actually there was no way that EATWOT women could have come together since Delhi. The Delhi assembly had decreed that the focus of EATWOT's work for the second five-year period would be regional rather than intercontinental. The sole exception was the First World-Third World dialogue, which had been envisioned since the Association's early days.[3] Entitled "Doing Theology in a Divided World," the gathering had for its purpose "to reflect on the meaning of our Christian faith in a divided and conflictual world"[4] so as to arrive at "a new methodology for doing theology that starts from commitment."[5]

It was a common commitment to struggle against all forms of oppression that bound the participants together despite the divisions among them in terms of their "World," color, gender, cultural background, and even expectations for the meeting.[6] There was no homogeneity in any of the groupings, whether among the First World participants or among the EATWOT members themselves. Among the latter, the regional emphases and differences which became evident in Delhi were just as pronounced in Geneva. Among the First World theologians, liberation theology also took a variety of accents. The conference statement specifically mentions feminist theology, theology of resistance, theology of conversion, theology of crisis, political theology, and radical evangelical theology.[7]

Among these theologies, feminist theology manifested itself as the most fully developed theology of liberation in the First World and created the greatest impact on the gathering. Though they did not speak with one voice, the feminist theologians from Europe and the United States formed an impressive and well-prepared group. While noting parallels between aspects of feminist theology and those of emerging Asian and African theologies,[8] the feminist theologians at the same time challenged the Third World male liberation theologians for their sexist language and patriarchal perspective.

Rosemary Radford Ruether's analysis[9] of the interrelatedness of oppression from a feminist perspective provoked a lengthy discussion on sexism, which became one of the major issues of the conference. Sexism clearly affects both women and men, for it concerns the basic fabric of human relationships in society. It was recognized that while male theologians may be progressive in their socio-political analyses and options, most have remained insensitive to gender oppression in their societies. Worse, the domination of women has been legitimated by Christian theology and official Church attitudes and practices.[10] Indeed, a notable breakthrough in Geneva was "the recognition that the sin of sexism is a universal system of marginalization of women that imposes further oppression on those already oppressed by poverty, race, and class in both First and Third Worlds."[11]

An additional session was granted in order to include the perspective of Third World women. This extra session, as well as the preparatory meeting for it, showed that while there were commonalities in the input of the women, there were also differences in their definition of issues and in approaches. For Third World women, sexism cannot be addressed apart from the total struggle for liberation in their countries. While they appreciated the need for inclusive language, this did not turn out to be a main concern for most of the Third World women whose mother tongues had few gender differentiated terms. It became evident in the course of the discussion that only Third World women themselves can define their agenda and priorities regarding women's oppression. Though dialogue with their First World sisters and their Third World brothers remains desirable, the conference statement put it succinctly when it declared that "neither Third World men nor First World women can determine the Third World women's agenda."[12]

On the whole, the women's performance in Geneva was significant not only in the issues they raised but also in those they supported.[13] The demand for a more comprehensive analysis, which was brought up by the Asian theologians and supported by the women, became a turning point in the conference. Class analysis is not enough. Just as important as the political and the economic categories are the religious and cultural in our critical analysis of reality. Moreover, because the dominant capitalist system is using *religious* language to legitimize its policies and to create its own idols, it became clear that "our understanding of the global system of domination will not be complete without a specifically theological analysis."[14]

The dialogue between First and Third World theologians ended with the admission that it was only a beginning. However, despite "the incomplete and all too fragmentary nature of our meeting," this initial dialogue offered "a ray of hope in a dark and divided world."[15] For EATWOT women, the dialogue provided an additional, and even brighter, ray of hope. It was at this time that the EATWOT Women's Commission was born.

### The Birthing Process

When the "irruption" occurred in Delhi, it precipitated the EATWOT women's resolve to do something about having Third World women's experience taken seriously.

It was clear to them that bonding was not enough, but it was not immediately evident what form their project should take. Some thought it should be a joint effort by men and women from the start; others felt that a focus on women by women was needed first. Only then could doing theology in the Third World be an inclusive, reciprocal, and egalitarian venture.

What was certain in Delhi was that EATWOT had to stop being a predominantly male enterprise, but it was only at the close of the

First World-Third World dialogue that EATWOT women were pro-
pelled to act decisively. Two factors influenced their move. First, the
session with the First World women made the Third World women
realize they were not clear about their own priorities; they needed to
organize themselves if they were to set their own agenda. Second, the
discussion on women's oppression called for a concrete and immediate response.

As members of EATWOT, the women knew that whatever they
decided on would need the approval of the executive committee,
whose annual meeting was scheduled at the end of the dialogue. The
women met briefly and agreed that a working commission within
EATWOT was the best route for them to take. They drew up a
proposal for a women's commission with a four-year program and
submitted it to the executive committee. The committee gave the
women's proposal its full approval, regarding it important to the
Association's overall efforts. Thus, on January 14, 1983, the Commission on Theology from Third World Women's Perspective became a
reality.[16]

Excited over the immediate approval of their program, the
EATWOT women lost no time in working towards its implementation.
The proposal gave as the main purpose of the Women's Commission
to promote a theology of liberation from the perspective of women in
the Third World, a theology that springs from a critical awareness of
women's subjugated position and a commitment to change it. Its
specific objectives thus included analyzing women's economic, political, cultural and religious realities within the Third World context,
as well as discerning the patriarchal elements in theology in order to
renew it. The proposal also outlined a progression of work in four
phases: from a national level in 1984, to a continental level in 1985, to
an intercontinental level in 1986 and finally, to an inter-world or global
level in 1987.

The first phase called for meetings on the national level which
involved both professional theologians and grass roots women from
different sectors of society. The aim of the national meetings was to
gain a deeper understanding of women's reality from the point of view
of women who experience oppression not only because of their
gender, but also because of their class, race, or ethnic origin.

The second phase designated continental consultations, with
the purpose of rereading Scripture from a new hermeneutic and
reworking theological themes on the basis of the lived experience of

African, Asian, and Latin American women. The list of theological themes included Christology, ecclesiology, Mariology, pneumatology (theology of the Holy Spirit), and spirituality.

In the third phase, there was to be an inter-continental conference to synthesize the work of the previous three years. In effect, this conference would summarize the experience and struggles, analysis and reflections, commitment and aspirations of Third World women.

The fourth and final phase was envisioned as a theological dialogue between Third World and First World women.

To carry out the Commission's four-phase program, it was important to find the right women for the different tasks. The principal one of overall supervision belonged to EATWOT's executive secretary as specified in the Constitution,[17] but just as pivotal was the coordination of the work on each of the Third World continents. Chosen to play this important role of continental coordinator were Marcy Amba Oduyoye for Africa, Sun Ai Lee Park for Asia, and Elsa Tamez for Latin America. These women were felicitous choices. All theologically-trained and dedicated to the ideals of EATWOT, they had the advantage of having experienced the "irruption" in Delhi and attending the dialogue in Geneva.

While the main responsibility of the continental coordinators was to organize the continental consultation in their respective areas, one of their other tasks was to find suitable contact persons for the national meetings. This was not an easy task, given the fact that in 1983, there were only twelve women among the fifty-eight EATWOT members: three from Africa, four from Asia, four from Latin America and one from the U.S. minorities. This meant having to locate contact persons outside the Association who were not only willing to organize the national meetings but also open to the EATWOT orientation.

### Implementing the Program

The implementation of the first phase of the program was not without complications. Besides the difficulty of finding suitable contact persons, there were problems of language and communication. Like the rest of EATWOT, the Commission had to operate in three languages: English, French, and Spanish; but most of the communication was done in English. Then there was the fact that not all the continental coordinators named were available to take on the

job.  Because Oduyoye was going to be away from Africa, she declined
assuming the role of coordinator.  It was not till 1985 that  Rose Zoe-
Obianga from Cameroun agreed to coordinate the African effort in
place of Oduyoye.  This not only delayed but also limited the work that
could be done in Africa for the first two phases of the program.

Despite delays and drawbacks, women on the three continents
forged ahead, eager to see the Commission's mandate accomplished.
The two years, 1984 and 1985, saw contact persons forming preparatory
committees, locating local theologians and grassroots women, and
inviting them to a "first" in most cases—a multi-sectoral gathering of
women to examine not only their reality but also their response to
their experience of double or even triple oppression in church and
society.  In Latin America, national meetings were held in Argentina,
Brazil, Peru and Central America. In Asia, women met in Hong Kong,
India, Japan, Korea, Malaysia, the Philippines, Sri Lanka, and New
Zealand.  In Africa, because of the many complications, only one
national meeting was held.  This was in Nigeria in 1985.

In most of the national meetings, women from peripheral
sectors of society were invited to share their experience as urban and
rural poor; as slum dwellers, factory workers, plantation laborers; as
members of tribal and indigenous communities; as wives of poor
fisherfolk and miners.  The exchange with these women was both a
stimulating and a sobering moment for the theologians. While they
noted similarities in their experience and struggle as women, there
were also significant differences. In the Philippines, for example,
while the major concern of the church women and women theologians was their identity as women, the chief concern of the women
from the impoverished and marginalized sectors was survival.  But
there was no doubt in the minds of the theologians that, in the end,
it is the women from the base who are best equipped to speak on Third
World women's reality, for they represent the majority of Third World
women.  There were variations in the way the national meetings were
carried out, but on the whole, those who attended them—EATWOT
members or not—felt these meetings were helpful in the work of
contextualizing theology from the viewpoint of Third World women.

### Organizing the Continental Consultations

*The Latin American Experience:*
The Women's Commission in Latin America was the first to plan

for the second phase of the proposed program. Towards the end of 1984, a group of contact persons met with Tamez in Bogota, Colombia, to organize the continental consultation in Latin America.[18] They were aware that preparations for the consultation had not been limited to the national meetings. There had also been, among other activities, reflection sessions with women in basic Christian communities in a number of Latin American countries, workshops on women and the Bible, study groups exploring women's spirituality, meetings with urban and rural women, and workshops on women's participation in church, society, and theology. There was also the collective work of women psychologists involved with basic Christian communities, and groups studying the theme of women and religious life.[19]

It was not surprising that those invited to the Latin American continental consultation consisted of a broad spectrum of women doing theology. Representing different Christian denominations, they were not only professors of theology, but also ordained ministers, religious sisters, historians, sociologists, researchers, and pyschologists. Because of the diversity of background and specialization, the planners decided to expand the list of themes contained in the original proposal to include other headings such as Women and Identity, Women and Life, Women and Popular Movements, and Women and the People of God. Each participant was assigned a topic according to her ministry or field of interest.[20]

Thus, from October 30 to November 3, 1985, twenty-seven women from nine countries of South and Central America and the Caribbean gathered in Buenos Aires, Argentina, "to share, from the woman's viewpoint, different aspects of the riches present in theology, reflecting the different ways this activity is carried out."[21]

The presentations were indeed rich and varied. Some of them explored issues that were also central to feminist theology in the United States, such as "women's spirituality, feminine aspect of the divine, women's way of ritualizing and celebrating, androcentric biases in the Bible and in the theological traditions, and women's experience across class, racial, cultural, and religious boundaries."[22] In a largely Christian context, the Latin American women showed daring in their theological effort by redefining women's religious experience to include cults and traditions like Candomble, which is an Afro-Brazilian mixture of traditional African and Catholic practices, and which has been branded by the Church as superstition. In Candomble, women are the religious leaders.[23]

Despite the variety of themes and approaches, the women at the Buenos Aires consultation were unanimous in affirming their roots in Latin American liberation theology. As Tamez admits, "within the last few years, other perspectives of God have appeared . . . (in) voices representing Asian, African, Black and Feminist theologies. As Latin American women we welcome these theologies; for ourselves, *adding women's perpective*, we claim Latin American liberation theology" (emphasis mine).[24]

This claim is evident in the papers and in the final statement. By making its point of departure the practice of liberation within the reality of poverty and exploitation on the continent, liberation theology does not separate the experience of oppression from the experience of God. From a women's perspective, liberation theology must incorporate women's concrete daily experience, and go beyond the "praxis of justice" and the life of faith, to include the "praxis of caring," that is, the need for collegial relations between men and women and among all peoples.[25] While affirming the contextual, communitarian, and militant nature of liberation theology, women must struggle against the machistic ideology so pervasive within their context, permeating their lives, their communities and institutions. Women need a "militant and combative theology . . . which gives them theological and biblical tools to tear out by the roots the sources of their marginalization."[26] As women identify themselves in the process of doing theology from women's perspective, they must be prepared "to leave behind the trappings with which society, the church and theology has dressed them,"[27] and to release themselves "from old frameworks and categories imposed by the patriarchal system."[28]

In their final statement, the Latin American women further characterized liberation theology from women's perspective as:

—unifying, bringing together different human dimensions;

—relational, bringing together a vast number of experiences so that people recognize themselves in this reflection and feel challenged by it;

—free, with the freedom of those who have nothing to lose; and open, capable of accepting different challenges and contributions;

—marked by a sense of humor, joy, and celebration, virtues that safeguard the certainty of faith in the God who is with us;

—filled with a spirituality of hope whose starting point is our situation as women, and which expresses strength, suffering, and thanksgiving.[29]

The tone of the Buenos Aires meeting was indeed inclusive and hope-filled. Though aware of the negative attitudes toward women and discriminatory practices against them in church and society, [30] the participants chose to focus on the achievements of women and their contribution to liberation theology. They sought to refashion women's history, recalling the many women in both biblical and contemporary times who, "acting out of their own situation, are symbols of struggle and resistance, wisdom and leadership, solidarity and fidelity, justice and peace."[31] There was a call to "join the feminist movement with popular movements" as well as to "invite our male colleagues to produce theology with us"[32] in order to help them "to see the strength and tenderness that are part of the common task of bringing forth and nourishing the life of the new person —woman/ man—and the new society."[33]

### *The Asian Experience:*

The Women's Commission in Asia began its continental consultation the very month the Latin American women ended theirs. The Asians chose Manila, Philippines, as the venue of their consultation; the dates, from November 21 to 30, 1985.

The Asian coordinator formed a planning committee to organize the meeting. Unlike the Latin American committee that was comprised of contact persons, the planning committee for Asia was made up of local church women and theologians.

Together with Lee Park, the Asian coordinator, seven women met in Manila on February 12-13, 1985, to plan the process and content of the consultation, which they envisioned as a working conference. They chose the over-all theme of "Total Liberation from Asian Women's Perspective" with the aim of articulating faith reflections on Asian reality for a more effective participation in the process of total liberation.[34] They agreed to use the original theological themes (with new titles) proposed by the Commission, and stated as the responsibility of each participant: (1) to write a paper on one of the topics listed, and (2) to prepare a biblical reflection on her national reality. Since analysis of the national reality was one of the main tasks in the first phase, the planners asked that attendance at a national meeting be a pre-condition for participation in the continental consultation. Each country was allotted three delegates.[35] Twenty-seven women[36] from seven different Asian countries and various Christian denominations assembled in Manila to share their reports and reflec-tions.[37] Process and atmosphere were two important components that facilitated the sharing. There was a relaxed atmosphere, with throw rugs and cushions strewn in the middle of the assembly hall so the participants could sit Asian style or recline as they chose.

The process entailed other activities besides the presentation and critique of papers. An "exposure" program, meant to give the participants first-hand experience of women's reality in the host country, included visits with "hospitality girls" in night clubs, with students and administrators of a socially-oriented women's college, with rural and urban poor women in fishing villages and picketlines, with missionary sisters, with middle-class professionals concerned with human rights, with feminist writers and journalists, and with affluent women in civic organizations.

A mural-painting session provided an alternate medium for expressing and deepening the participants' analysis of women's reality and their theological insights on woman. The resulting murals, together with the stories the women shared, showed that despite the diversity of cultures and traditions, Asian women suffered common oppressions, which the conference statement verbalized as follows:

> In all spheres of Asian society, women are dominated, dehuman-ized and dewomanized; they are discriminated against, exploited, harassed, sexually used, abused and viewed as inferior beings who must always subordinate themselves to the so-called male supremacy. In the home, church, law, education and media, women have been treated with bias and condescension. In Asia and all over the world, the myth of the subservient, servile Asian woman is blatantly peddled to reinforce the dominant male stereotype image.[38]

The major part of the process was the study and discussion of biblical reflections and theological papers.[39] The biblical reflections were presented and critiqued in plenary. However, for study of the theological papers, participants were grouped according to the theme they had written on. After individual study of the papers, they were discussed in the small groups, with the objective of producing a "composite paper" on the theme.

This part of the process proved difficult and confusing for the participants. While it was meant to highlight the collective character of doing Third World women's theology, the writing of composite papers almost evoked a mini-revolt. It was not until the purpose—as well as the expected result—of the composite paper was clarified that the conference could move on. A composite paper was not, as some thought, pieces taken from each prepared paper on a theme and put together. Nor should it end up, which some feared, as a watered-down version of what the delegates had painstakingly written back home. Rather a composite paper should be a qualitatively new product created in synergetic fashion from the best insights from the group. In the end, the evaluation of the conference revealed that for all the participants, the struggle to produce a common paper despite differences was an enriching experience.[40] The final statement summarizes this experience as follows: "In our theologizing, we attempted a creative and collective work style, which we felt mirrored the vision of that community toward which we are striving . . . In the process we uncovered hidden realities and arrived at conclusions.[41]

Some of these common conclusions were summarized in the final statement. The following are a few excerpts:

—Oppression of women is sinful. This systemic sin is rooted in organized and established economic, political, and cultural structures with patriarchy as an overarching and all-pervading reality that oppresses women.

—The highly patriarchal churches have definitely contributed to the subjugation and marginalization of women.

—Theology itself has added to these distortions . . . Theological premises, traditions, and beliefs . . . have blurred the image of God that we are.

—The bias against women in Christian tradition (is) buttressed by male-oriented Asian religious beliefs.[42]

Just as in the process the women "uncovered hidden realities" that have diminished women in Asia, so, in the experience together, they rediscovered empowering elements of their Christian faith: Jesus' liberating and salvific mission that encompasses all, his radical breakthroughs and supportive stance for women, the Holy Spirit's bonding presence that overcomes the divisive forces of death and evil, the true Mary of the Gospels who identifies, and *is,* with today's grieving mothers, wives, and daughters in the bitter fight for freedom.[43] In their encounter with the poor in the picketlines and in the countryside, they encountered the Christ of the poor, the Christ of women, who are the poorest of the poor.

As the conference came to a close, the women declared anew

their solidarity with all oppressed people, most expecially women, in the painful struggle for full humanity. They denounced all forms of evil that subjugate women and renewed their support for women's movements in confronting patriarchal structures and traditions. They resolved to promote authentic feminist education and the development of a liberating theology from the perspective of Asian women. They called for unity and solidarity beyond gender and race, for "it is only by working together toward a new community of women and men that the world will witness the coming of the new Kingdom, which is the embodiment of justice, equality, peace, and love.[44]

### The African Experience:

The Women's Commission in Africa had a slow and circuitous start. Zoe-Obianga was still in France finishing a post-graduate course when she received the appeal to take on the coordinatorship of the women's program in Africa. She was aware of the problems of getting African women together for a continental consultation. There was a language barrier between the English-speaking and the French-speaking women theologians and no existing network of Protestant and Catholic women. There were poor communications and travel connections between countries. Yet Zoe-Obianga did not want African women any less prepared for the intercontinental dialogue than their Asian and Latin American sisters. Upon her return to Cameroun, she sought and found a creative and economical way of having the African women meet, namely, to make use of a projected African EATWOT regional meeting for the women's gathering.

Together, Zoe-Obianga and regional coordinator Mveng devised a joint project for EATWOT in Africa. It would combine the regional meeting of EATWOT members with the consultation of the Women's Commission. Twenty men and twenty women were slated to meet in Cairo, Egypt, from August 24 to 28, 1985, to study two themes: "Spirituality and Liberation in Africa," chosen by the African membership, and "Men and Women Building Together the Church in Africa," chosen by the Women's Commission.[45] Unfortunately, for a variety of reasons—whether personal, communicational, or organizational—only seventeen attended the meeting, and among them, only three women. Zoe-Obianga herself failed to attend due to an unexpected tragedy in the family.

Zoe-Obianga had to think of another way of getting African women together while avoiding the high cost of extensive travel and the added expense of interpreters. The solution was to have two continental consultations, one for the francophones and another for the anglophones. On August 3-9, 1986, thirty francophone women from Cameroun, Rwanda, Madagascar, and Zaire, met in Yaounde, Cameroun.[46] On August 19-23, 1986, thirty-three anglophone women from Ghana, Kenya, Nigeria, and Sierra Leone, gathered in Port Harcourt, Nigeria;[47] Zoe-Obianga and four part-time male participants also attended the Port Harcourt meeting.

The Yaounde meeting had an exceptional significance for the French-speaking African women for it was their first meeting together under the auspices of EATWOT. Ten women presented papers on women in relation to the church, the Bible, theology, Christology, spirituality, and the struggle for liberation. The presentations and subsequent discussions in plenary and in groups proved enlightening and enriching. The consultation highlighted for them some beliefs and convictions: that the Bible needs to be reread with "women's eyes", that women must claim their rightful place in society and in the church for this will never be given them as a gift, that the church cannot live apart from the world but must remain open and attentive to concrete human situations.[48] The church should study the deep significance of African rituals and search new ways of expressing them in the initiation to Christian life in Africa. Because African women are "the soul of society and thus the initiating teacher in spiritual and divine matters,"[49] they must be prepared by the church to preach the Word of God, to direct retreats and small groups, as well as to take responsibility for the formation of . . . lay leaders, apostolic workers, priests, and other ordained persons. Moreover, both lay and religious women should be given responsible positions in the administration of the church and the management of its resources. Hopefully, the church would seriously study how women in Africa could participate in the administration of salvation through the sacraments.

The continental consultation of anglophone African women held in Port Harcourt in 1986 was organized by Teresa Okure, who the year before had cooordinated the national meeting in Nigeria. The consultation was a fruitful one. In particular, it gave the women new spectacles with which to read the Bible, giving them "new insights which we hope will lead us to a holistic understanding of what it means to be church in Africa today."[50] In their conference communique, they made several affirmations and commitments. They affirmed that:

—men and women together image God and that *neither* is complete without the other;

—in Christ is seen the fullness of true humanity; thus Christianity in Africa should be a force for full human development;

—women have a vital contribution to make in God's project in bringing all God's children to full humanity.[51]

Consequently, the women committed themselves to:

—participate in the holistic human development that will eliminate the life-denying forces in church and society, especially those rooted in ritual;

—work toward eliminating racism, abject poverty, and the neglect of rural areas;

—work together with other women and cooperate with all who seek to promote Christ's message in all its fullness.[52]

The women who met in Port Harcourt aspired to break the silence that had restricted women's participation in decisions that affect their lives, and called upon people of good will to join forces with women in working for total liberation and transformation of African men and women through the power of the gospel.[53]

By the end of August, 1986, all three continents had completed the second phase of the women's program. Earlier, a continental coordinator had remarked that "it was an exciting experience to be a coordinator . . . I saw how country groupings creatively used the guideline and gave different characters to it."[54] This creative use of the guideline was true of the continental consultations as well. The consultations might not have produced anything that was never said before; the important thing was that Third World women were now able to speak their theological word and be heard. And the force of their voice was growing.

# CHAPTER FOUR

## THE "OAXTEPEC ENCOUNTER" AND AFTER

The continental consultations paved the way for the intercontinental conference, which marked the third phase of the EATWOT women's program. Involving three continents in a single activity required more careful planning and coordination. Actually, before all the consultations were completed, preparations for the tricontinental meeting of Third World women theologians had already started.

### The Women's Double Preparation

According to the original proposal of the Women's Commission, the intercontinental conference was scheduled for 1986. This was also the year of EATWOT's second general assembly, the planning for which had started two years before. The executive committee had chosen Mexico as the venue, and the first week of December 1986 as the time for the assembly. A preparatory meeting for this EATWOT event was scheduled for February 7-10, 1986, in Mexico City.

With this in view, the program coordinator and the executive secretary studied the advantages of having the women's tricontinental meeting around the same time and in the same place as the general assembly. Subsequently, the decision was made to hold the women's conference from December 1 to 4, 1986, in Mexico City. Because some of the same women were expected to attend the preparatory meeting for the assembly as well, the planning session for the women's conference was conveniently set for February 5-6, 1985, in

Mexico City.[1]

The planners decided to keep the overall task and theme, "Doing Theology from Third World Women's Perspective," and to retain the general objectives suggested for the continental consultations:

—to broaden our understanding of women's situation in our respective socioeconomic, political, and religio-cultural realities;

—to discover the vital aspects of women's experience of God in emerging spiritualities;

—to reread the Bible from (a) Third World women's perspective in the light of total liberation;

—to articulate faith reflections on women's realities, struggles, and spirituality;

—to deepen our commitment and solidarity work toward full humanity for all.[2]

To achieve these objectives, the planners chose to use the original theological themes and proposed the following as titles for the conference papers: "The Reality of Oppression and Struggle of Women," "The Vital Aspects of Women's Experience of God in Emerging Spiritualities," "Women and the Church," "Women and Theology," "Women and the Bible," and "Women and Christology."[3] There would be ten participants from each continent,[4] some of whom would be assigned to prepare papers. However, all EATWOT women were expected to be involved in the preparation.

The women's planning session in February 1985, was immediately followed by the preparatory meeting for the EATWOT assembly. At the preparatory meeting, it was decided to follow through on an executive committee suggestion that the Women's Commission write a paper on EATWOT from the women's perspective. Thus besides participating in the general preparations for the assembly, the EATWOT women would be asked to prepare a critique of EATWOT, its work and processes, to be presented at the general assembly itself.

The EATWOT women did not mind the double preparation; in fact, they welcomed it. The additional assignment from the preparatory committee implied that, at last, the Association was ready to listen to its women members and to take their presence and contribution seriously. Two years before, some of the male members complained when the executive committee introduced a change in the membership policy in favor of the women. The committee had noted the numerical discrepancy between the male and female members within EATWOT,[5] and made the decision that at least one third of the members in each region should be women. This ratio would also hold for the elected officers of the Association. For some male members, this new policy would impede EATWOT's growth, for there would not be "enough qualified women" in the regions to fill the required ratio.

Aware that the "numbers game" was not sufficient proof of a redirection of EATWOT's male-centered orientation, the women members were nevertheless pleased with the attempts to have more women take active role in the Association's major activities. For instance, the assembly preparatory committee, made up of an equal number of women and men,[6] stipulated that for the assembly itself, at least one third of the participants should be women. Moreover, any woman invited to the intercontinental women's conference would also be welcome to attend the assembly, *whether or not* she was part of the regional quota. When EATWOT members actually gathered in Mexico in December 1986, women constituted over forty per cent of the assembly.[7]

## The Oaxtepec Encounter [8]

When the site of the EATWOT assembly was later moved from Mexico City to Oaxtepec, the women's local support committee made the corresponding change. Thus it was in Oaxtepec, Mexico, that twenty-six women theologians gathered to share the fruit of their common endeavor: eight from Africa, nine from Asia, and nine from South and Central America. There were nine Protestants and seventeen Catholics. To these twenty-six women also belonged the task of discerning the similarities and differences in their theological approaches and priorities as Third World women.

The participants agreed that Mexico provided the proper backdrop for theological reflection from the perspective of Third World women—Mexico, "where an affluent minority and a poor majority exist side by side, where signs of its colonial past and neocolonial present are everywhere evident, where machismo' is still a given." [9] Moreover, the vacation center in Oaxtepec where the conference was held, with its scenic spots and spacious grounds, offered the appropriate atmosphere for both serious study and relaxed camaraderie.

The mood was set as Tamez gave her word of welcome to the delegates on behalf of the hosting group, the Latin American women. Her introductory talk included a reflection on the Levite's nameless concubine in Judges 19.[10] The concubine did not speak out against the oppression meted out to her, but her cut-up body did. All who saw the outcome of this atrocity were enjoined "to consider it, take counsel, and speak out" (19:30). As a result, Israel got up as one and stood united to act for justice.[11]

Tamez's brief but poignant reflection served to motivate the delegates to act as one in pondering the oppression of women, discussing it, and giving their verdict. Although it was the first time most of the women met each other and some had to communicate through interpreters, an earnest, congenial, and collaborative spirit became immediately evident, a spirit that was manifest not only in the formal sessions, but also in the worship services and social activities. Throughout the conference, one sensed a united effort to make the Commission's first tricontinental theological venture a success.

The initial session dealt with the reality of oppression and the struggle of women. One after the other, delegates from the three continents who were assigned this topic recounted women's inferior status in the economic, social, political, cultural, racial, religious, and even in the familial realms of life. While Third World women experience discrimination and exploitation in varying forms and degrees, they are all victims of the same web of domination of which sexism is a major part.

Third World women, however, have stopped seeing themselves simply as victims or even just quietly accepting their lot. Becoming more conscious of their oppression as women, they have started to band together and organize liberating movements and projects, some of which are motivated by Christian faith.[12]

Christian women see their efforts rooted in faith and Scripture, believing that "being created in God's image demands a total rupture with the prevailing patriarchal system in order to build a just society."[13] Together with other Third World women, they concur that this task is "deeply connected with the efforts of all the poor and the oppressed who are struggling for their liberation in all aspects of life."

While the delegates shared these common viewpoints, they were at the same time aware of differences in the liberation process taking place in the three continents. In their final document, they reported:

> In Latin America, women organize themselves around survival strategies. In Africa, the rebirth of women takes place in their

struggle to overthrow the oppressive elements in traditional African cultures and religions and the evils of colonialism. In Asia, the struggle is centered in rediscovering the pride of being woman, in building womanhood and humane communities, and in fighting against political, economic, and sexual injustices.

The final document also contains highlights from the discussion of the other conference themes. The deliberation on emerging spiritualities revealed many commonalities. Third World women's spirituality and theologizing are intertwined, both arising from their experience of being discriminated against as women and as people of the Third World. The conference delegates proclaimed: "The emerging spiritualities we perceive in the three continents show that spiritual experience rooted in action for justice constitutes an integral part of our theology. . . Spiritual experience for women in the Third World thus means being in communion with all who fight for life." They see compassion and solidarity as main elements of their spirituality and theology, expressed in organized, patient and loving action. The variation in the action is due "to religious and cultural differences among the continents, to the diversities within the various regions in each continent, and to the varied ways the different churches assimilate these new experiences." One commonality that surfaced in the three presentations on this theme was the ecumenical nature of the emerging spiritualities, not only among various Christian groups, but also between Christians and people of other faiths and beliefs.[14]

With regard to the topic, "Women and the Bible," there was consensus that Scripture "plays a vital role in the lives of women and in our struggle for liberation."[15] At the same time, it was recognized that women face the constant challenge of interpreting texts that are against them. Such texts should be considered in their cultural contexts and epochs, "not as normative, but as peripheral and not touching the heart of the gospel. The essentially patriarchal nature of the Bible and the interpretations that reinforce the oppressive elements should be acknowledged and exposed."[16]

The participants in Oaxtepec felt no need to reject the Bible, as some women do. Instead, they advocated "mining" deeper into it, giving prominence to those parts which portray women as agents of life, as well as those which demonstrate Jesus' respectful relationship with women that ran counter to the practice of his time. Such biblical passages have proved a source of empowerment for Third World women.

Though the participants in Oaxtepec belonged to different Christian denominations, the discussion on "Women and the Church" showed many common concerns. "Our strong faith and numerous services of love keep the church alive, especially among the poor and the marginalized. Yet though we constitute a strong labor force . . . we are powerless and voiceless, and in most churches are excluded from leadership roles and ordained ministries." This reprehensible situation called for new ways of being church that reflected more truly God's reign and the new creation. As the women expressed in their final document:

> Our faith in the power of the cross and the resurrection empowers us to live out the vision of God's new creation, where no one is subordinated or enslaved, but where free people take part in God's liberating project to build a true community and a new society. . . In all Third World continents, the presence of women who stand for justice in all its forms is both challenging and conflictive. But this is the way in which the church will be able to rediscover its true identity.

The next topic considered, Christology, emerged as central to Third World women's theology. While the women of the three continents equally affirmed that it is in the person and praxis of Jesus Christ that they find the ground of their liberation from all discrimination and alienation, nevertheless, they saw the need to contextualize Christology "in the oppressed and painful realities of our continents." They saw Christology as "integrally linked with action on behalf of social justice and the defense of each person's right to life and to a more humane life."[17] Thus, if Christology is to be contextualized, then it has to relate to the causes of people's suffering and misery as well as to the efforts for justice as they are experienced in the Third World. This means that in Africa, Christology has to do with apartheid, racial discrimination, militarism, deficiency syndromes that come in foreign-aid packages, and genocide perpetrated through family-planning programs. In Asia, with the massive poverty, sexual exploitation, and racial, ethnic, caste, and religious discrimination, Christology incorporates the efforts to draw out humanizing elements in other religions. In Latin America, where poverty and oppression often give rise to a tendency to use religion to reinforce a passive and fatalistic attitude to life, Christology is necessarily connected with the preferential option for the poor.[18]

There was a lengthy discussion on suffering in relation to Christology, for people in the three continents, especially the women, have a great devotion to the passion and cross of Jesus. They associate Jesus' suffering with their own, but often without the awareness that it is only suffering undergone for the sake of God's reign or resulting from the uncontrollable and mysterious conditions of nature and humankind that has salvific value. It was bringing forth new life that gave meaning to Jesus' passion, death and resurrection. Suffering inflicted by the oppressor and passively accepted is nonredeeming and even destructive.[19]

Methodology was dealt with in conjunction with Christology, for key to the theology done by Third World women is the word *life*. In doing theology, women in the three continents find themselves committed to all the vital elements that compose human life. Thus without losing its scientific seriousness, which includes analyzing the roots of women's multiple oppression, their theologizing is grounded in experience, in affection, in life. Their theology is done with passion and compassion,[20] based on feeling as well as on knowledge, on wisdom as well as on science, done not only with the mind, but also with the heart, the body, the womb.[21] This theology is articulated not only in words, but also in prayer and worship, in the relationship with the neighbor in whom God lives, and in the ongoing struggle in solidarity with the poor and the oppressed.[22] This has repercussions not only on women's theology but on all theology.

The emerging Third World women's theology is thus people-oriented, but it "goes beyond the personal to encompass the community, and beyond gender to embrace humanity in all its integrity."[23] Its aim is the liberation of all women and men from whatever binds them both internally and externally, and liberation means wholeness. Hence the emerging theology done by Third World women is necessarily liberational in its intent, collective and ecumenical in its approach, and inclusive in its perspective and goal.[24]

The evaluation of the women's intercontinental conference showed that the delegates were satisfied with the "encounter" and the outcome. They also appreciated the variation in the dynamics that included role-playing, audio-visual presentations, a fishbowl session, small group discussions, and mural painting.

As the meeting began, so it ended with a scriptural reflection on a woman. This time it was the woman in John 12 who anointed Jesus' feet with costly perfume:

> This woman's action is a passionate and compassionate action—
> passionate, because by anointing Jesus with so expensive a
> perfume, she shows her extreme love for him; compassionate,
> because her action gives Jesus the opportunity to direct the
> community's attention to the poor and to exhort solidarity with
> them.[25]

As the woman, by her loving gesture, spread fragrance throughout the house, so Third World women are called to do likewise. By committing themselves to do a passionate and compassionate theology, they shall spread the fragrance of the Good News throughout the earth.[26]

### EATWOT's Oaxtepec Assembly

At the close of the women's conference, seventeen of them stayed on to attend EATWOT's second general assembly. The theme was "The Commonalities and Divergences among Third World Theologies." Though the assembly was held in the same venue, to the women who participated in the previous conference the contrast was striking. The spirit was different. It seemed that competition instead of collaboration prevailed. There was friction among the men from different regions, and signs of frustration and dissatisfaction. In her reflection on the Oaxtepec assembly, Maria Clara Bingemer observed: "As the assembly progressed, there were difficulties and conflicts, produced by divisions and misunderstandings within our number."[27] But in the end, the desire to resolve the tensions so as to achieve the assembly objectives won out.

The assembly experience seemed to mirror some of the situations in the Third World. Bingemer describes the Third World theologians who assembled in Oaxtepec as people who "clearly felt they all came from countries under attack: on the economic, social, political, ideological, and cultural fronts."[28] Unlike the five years prior to the 1981 EATWOT assembly, which were hopeful years for the Third World,[29] the years 1981-1986 were grim and difficult ones. The previous optimism had slowly waned as the First World nations regained their control of the international situation. Sadly enough, this triumph of the First World can be largely attributed to the grip it has on the elite of the Third World, who believe in First World ideologies and schemes, and run repressive governments for the benefit of a world oligarchy. This has resulted in worsening poverty, large-scale oppression, and the spiraling of external debts.[30] The unfavorable effect of all this on women was noted in particular at the close of the UN Decade for Women and Development in 1985.[31]

It was not only Third World countries under attack; Third World Christians involved in liberation efforts were themselves under attack on two fronts: by the secular powers and by the administrative powers of Christian institutions which had become suspicious of Third World movements, liberation theology, and basic church communities. Confronted with opposition and risks, it was not easy to be a theologian in the Third World.[32]

Although the objectives of the assembly were not fully realized, commonalities, differences, and the fruit of cross-fertilization among Third World theologies were surfaced. Besides the same overall purpose of these theologies, three main common elements were clearly present.[33] First, Third World theologies arise from spiritual experience and contemplative commitment. Born of suffering and humiliation on the one hand, and of the longing for dignity and wholeness on the other, they pose the hard choice: to serve the God of life or worship the idol of gold. Second, Third World theologies are "combative" theologies which "attempt to introduce theological discourse within the movement of peoples organizing themselves for their liberation."[34] Third, they are also ecclesial theologies, rooted in the church, despite differences in denomination, in regional and cultural expression, in involvement in the process of liberation, and in response to situations of challenge.

Like the commonalities that were surfaced, the divergences that emerged were not entirely new. Latin America appeared as the most influenced by Westernized Christianity. Thus for a long time, its theologians had minimalized popular religiosity and ignored the native and Afro-based religious values in their midst. Asia and Africa were more similar in that they did theology in a multireligious context. As stated in the Oaxtepec document, "the living religions of Africa and Asia call for a conscious incorporation of theologies other than Christian into our thinking."[35] It was Asia, however, that posed some crucial questions to the assembly: Is Jesus of Nazareth the whole of the Christ, the whole Word of God? Is not the reality of Jesus larger than the particular flesh-history he lived? With regard to Scripture, they asked: Could a live historical process and spiritual quest be ruled forever by fixed texts born of particular, limited experiences of one ancient group of people?[36]

It was obvious that the dialogue within EATWOT should continue.[37] While the assembly was primarily a forum for exchange, it also became an opportunity for self-criticism. At the close of the time together, there was deeper awareness and greater respect for each one's "otherness;" the women sensed a greater openness among the male members especially as the women presented their assessment of EATWOT.

While appreciating the advances made by the Association with respect to the incorporation of more women into its activities, membership, and official positions, the women asked that this be done not simply because of their feminine gender but because of their theological competence and leadership capability.[38] Among other recommendations, they asked that the male members include the women's viewpoint in their work so that Third World theology becomes more global and inclusive.[39] As a result, an entire section of the Oaxtepec document was dedicated to the women's theological perspective and contribution, gleaned mostly from the conclusions of the women's intercontinental conference. The attempt was appreciated, but what the women were after was not just more space in documents or to complement or deepen men's theology, but "to change the whole style of doing theology."[40]

### After Oaxtepec

The five years after the Intercontinental Conference and the second EATWOT assembly were spent in regional work, both in terms of the Association and the Women's Commission. There was only one exception: the Third World women's dialogue with the U.S. minority women in Atlanta from May 3 to 8, 1989. Attended by ten women from the Third World and seven from the U.S. minorities, the dialogue was meant for sharing experiences and discovering commonalities and differences that affect the way Third World women from different contexts do theology. Some striking commonalities emerged, among which were "a cosmology in which creation is sacred" and "the importance of doing theology *with* the community."[41]

There would have been a second exception, namely, the dialogue between First World and Third World women theologians but this was rescheduled. It was to be the fourth and culminating phase of the

Commission's program drawn up in Geneva, but this activity was postponed till after the third EATWOT general assembly in 1992.

In the meantime, the EATWOT women were busily involved in the Association's regional activities. The African women were part of a number of mini-consultations held in different countries as preparation for the EATWOT African Continental Conference which took place in Harare, Zimbabwe, in January 1991. Some of the EATWOT women were speakers or panelists in that regional event.

A number of the Latin American women are engaged in an EATWOT-related project to publish a multi-volume work on liberation theology. Together with EATWOT men, they are also involved in theological and pastoral reflection in relation to the Santo Domingo conference in 1992, which was to coincide with the 500th anniversary of the colonization and evangelization of the Americas. This coincidence caused much doubt about the ambiguous process of evangelization that has been linked with the shortcomings of colonization.

In Asia, EATWOT women were resource persons at the initial meeting of the Theological Study Commission. This consultation on religion and liberation was held in New Delhi in 1987. Asian EATWOT women were also among the forty participants of the Third Asian Theological Conference (ATC III) held near Seoul, Korea, in July of 1989. Entitled "An Asian Search for a Liberation Spirituality,"[42] this event was the first in EATWOT history that could boast of an equal number of male and female participants. It was also the first time that the men and women of EATWOT openly discussed the subject of sexuality as an inherent part of spirituality.[43] In January of 1991, three EATWOT women joined their male colleagues in Hong Kong for a mini-consultation on Christology in preparation for the 1992 general assembly. When the Asian region was assigned the Christology paper for the assembly, the Asian EATWOT members agreed it should be a collective effort that would include a variety of Asian perspectives, including Asian women's. While EATWOT women actively contributed to these regional events, nevertheless, they had activities of their own to further the work of developing theology from a Third World women's perspective.

### In Africa:

Two activities involved the African members of the Women's Commission during the post-Oaxtepec years: (1) the formal convocation of the Circle of Concerned African Women Theologians in 1989 and (2) the meeting of African women in Zimbabwe in 1991 in preparation for EATWOT's third general assembly.

EATWOT members had a leading role in convoking the Circle of Concerned African Women Theologians, which had been in existence for several years but was formally established in 1989.[44] The Circle considers itself an "ever expanding group" of women, with or without formal education in theology, bound together in their common belief that religion and culture are key in the liberation of the humanity of women.[45] Past research projects on "women and development" have often exposed cultural factors "without associating them with religious beliefs and myths that rule women's lives and hamper women's development."[46] It was thus fitting that the Circle's first activity was the inauguration of the biennial Institute of African Women in Religion and Culture. Designed to bring women together to study, share, write, and publish theological literature during a seven-year period, the Institute also projects national meetings and mid-session conferences following the initial convocation in 1989. Because this involves local and sectoral Circles, in effect, the Institute liaises the African EATWOT women with other women theologians on the continent in this undertaking.[47]

The first Institute brought together close to seventy women, with EATWOT women comprising most of the International Planning Committee. Each day focussed on a specific issue in religion and culture, under the overarching theme and rallying cry, "Daughters of Africa, Arise." It was obvious from the start "that the African woman, no matter where she is on the continent, was and is oppressed by both religion and culture."[48] In the presentations and workshops, African rituals and marital customs such as polygamy loomed large not only as cultural and religious issues but as crucial theological issues as well. Since the motif of death and life are found in all African rituals, those that renew life and enhance one's humanity should be retained, while those that degrade women, such as some puberty, widowhood, and purification rites, should be dropped.

In discussing the plight of African women in relation to culture and religion, the participants recognized that their problems were "also of a political nature . . . Our private hurts are public issues linked with how women as a whole are treated . . . That is why we must name it sexism."[49] In the struggle against sexism women must make their own models of development and of womanhood. And they must strive to liberate all those "captured by sexism"—the gospel and the church included.[50]

As the first Institute coincided with the beginning of the WCC-sponsored Ecumenical Decade of Churches in Solidarity with Women, the Circle members saw themselves raising theological issues around the Decade and making a special contribution to it. However, they acknowledged that their "struggle to demand the recognition of the image of God in woman will be undermined as long as women exploit women and succumb to hierarchical thinking."[51]

Worship life and Bible studies were integral to the Institute. Together with the issue plenaries and workshops, the total experience was a stimulating, inspiring and healing one for the women. It was a hope-filled beginning.[52] If the production of theological literature was the Institute goal and priority, then the first Institute was indeed a success: more than fifty essays were written.[53]

The second activity involving the EATWOT women in Africa was the preparatory conference organized by the Commission's African coordinator, Marie-Bernadette Mbuy-Beya. Because of the political situation in Zaire during the latter half of 1991, Mbuy-Beya shifted the venue of the conference to Zimbabwe. From November 19 to 22, 1991, representatives fom Kenya, Namibia, Zimbabwe, Nigeria, Uganda, Tanzania, and Zaire gathered in Harare to discuss the conference theme: "Third World Spirituality—A Cry for Life."

The women affirmed the Gospel's message of liberation for women which helps to "discern between the positive and negative values contained in tradition and culture."[54] At the same time, they felt that research on the traditional religions was necessary to "discover the richness which can be integrated into an authentic Christian experience and play a vital role in African spirituality."[55] The women also stressed the importance of liturgy and the consequent need to "invent symbols which speak to the heart of Africans." Moreover, they encouraged the use of a methodology "which allows room for our struggle and cry as women."

As EATWOT members, the women recognized the difficulty of communication and exchanges among them[56] and urged one another to find access to mass media as well as to publish their writings. At the end of the conference, they issued messages for the Churches and peoples of Africa: church leaders, ministers, religious women, married women, as well as people in political institutions. Their general demand was for justice and liberation and for greater participation in decision-making that affects women's lives. They also had a word for all EATWOT members: "to work together for the restoration of the face of God in the midst of humanity."[57] In this regard, they reminded EATWOT women that "the best struggle is one that is led by women and men together to help improve the status of women both in religion and in the culture."[58]

*In Latin America:*
   The Latin American women, in the person of Tamez, had a series of interviews with ten women from the continent. It was a sequel to the dialogue with male liberation theologians on the subject of "women" conducted by Tamez in 1986.[59] While the two projects were not EATWOT-sponsored, Tamez acknowledged that the idea for doing the interviews with liberation theologians came from her experience of dialogue within EATWOT. The women's responses to the interview questions were rich and varied, showing different levels of consciousness and areas of feminist concerns. This verified the need for continuing a reflective dialogue not only with their male colleagues but among Latin American women themselves.
   In her introduction to *Las mujeres toman la palabra*, which contains the interviews with the women, Tamez makes four observations regarding the women's responses. In the first place, it is clear that the category of class is necessary but not sufficient for an analysis of "women." Reflecting on poor women implies speaking of women who are also oppressed because of their gender. In past discussions, this was quickly passed over to move on to the subject of economically-oppressed women, that is, women as victims of the capitalist system. In the second place, there is the need to study feminist theories as tools of analysis, not only for understanding the oppression of women but also for developing a more coherent and effective theology from women's perspective. According to Tamez, this is a definite breakthrough for Latin American women some of whom had objected to feminists for not showing enough interest in social change on a global level. Some of those interviewed said that past prejudices should be put aside and feminist theories from all parts of the world studied by both female and male theologians, reinterpreting and reworking them if necessary. In the third place, it was surprising that some spoke very openly of women's ordination, especially as a vital concern of basic ecclesial communities. This topic was not given much attention in the past. Finally, there is the need for clarifying and

deepening what is meant by "a women's perspective" as well as by the term "feminine." Both can be misunderstood and misused to the detriment of women. What is clear to the Latin American women is that the theology they are trying to develop is not a "feminine" theology but rather a theology from a women's point of view *(desde la optica de la mujer)*. This view includes woman's experience of oppression in history as well as her contribution as "the other," as a different being *(como un ser diferente)*. What it means to be different still needs further exploration and definition. Nevertheless, women's point of view should be present in all theology and hermeneutics, as well as in the church itself.[60]

### In Asia:

The Asian EATWOT women had a two-part consultation on Asian women's hermeneutics, the first part held in Seoul, Korea in 1989, the second in Madras, India in 1990. Earlier, in November of 1987, the Women's Commission in Asia cosponsored with the Asian Women's Resource Centre for Culture and Theology a conference on "Asian Women Doing Theology," which took place in Singapore.[61]

The Seoul consultation was held at the Marist Retreat Center from June 30 to July 2, 1989, just prior to the Asian EATWOT event often referred to as ATC III.[62] Though it was the first meeting intended primarily for the Asian EATWOT women as a group, there was an immediate bonding established among them. Unfortunately not all the Asian EATWOT women could attend the consultation, and only five countries were represented.

The complexity and diversity that is Asia was reflected from the planning stages of the consultation. Though the planners all subscribed to the EATWOT methodology in doing theology, the similarity practically ended there. There were obvious differences among them in terms of expectations, approach, use of terms, and choice of process and content. In a letter to the Asian EATWOT women in May of 1988, Lee Park proposed having three main topics for the three-day consultation, which she delineated as follows: "(1) Analysis of patriarchy as it is manifested in our national reality; (2) Asian women's critical hermeneutical principles as I use them in my work; and (3) historical analysis of Jesus' time: international dimension, internal political, economic and religious power dynamics." She suggested having each participant write a paper on each of the three topics, to be discussed in "a participatory type of workshop" and "formulated as group consensus."

It soon became obvious that there were other views about the consultation. Some felt the proposed plan was too ambitious for a three-day meeting. A few thought that each of the topics was enough for a separate consultation by itself. Moreover, writing three papers on three broad and complex topics was too much to ask of anyone, and discussing so many papers in the workshops would preclude any meaningful exchange among the participants.

Lee Park adjusted her position, and narrowed down the themes to two: "Patriarchy in our Asian Reality" and "Asian Women's Hermeneutical Principle on the Basis of our Reality." Each participant was only asked to write a single paper combining the two themes, but making the connections clear.

When the day of the consultation arrived, the sixteen delegates came forth with essays on patriarchy, but only the Philippine delegates completed the assignment on hermeneutical principles. And this was possible only because the Philippine delegates decided to work together and write a composite paper on the subject.[63] In the discussion following the Philippine presentation, it became obvious there were different understandings as to what constituted a hermeneutical principle. The consultation statement was found wanting on this score, so Lee Park called a luncheon meeting to revise the draft. However, not all could attend this meeting during which it was agreed to state the principle as follows:

—Search for God-provided ways of liberation, starting from our experience of oppression as women and (as) Asians;
—Dialogue between our own texts of life and the scriptural texts;
—Foster the message of equality, unity, justice and peace in all personal and social relationships;
—Rediscover the power of women and people in our traditional cultures and religions;
—Promote relationships of sharing and mutuality between women and men;
—Nurture, care (for) and protect creation.

The two Philippine delegates tasked with editing the draft felt that methodology had been mixed in with the hermeneutical principle, and took it upon themselves to invite the other Philippine delegates to restudy the draft in light of the consultation material and experience. Together they worked on a new revision and restated the emerging Asian women's hermeneutical principle as follows:

We interpret as in accord with God's design for full humanity and authentic womanhood, and with the Spirit's action in history
—whatever promotes genuine dialogue among people of different cultures, religions and ideologies;
—whatever fosters equality, unity, justice and peace in all personal and social relationships;
—whatever empowers women and other marginalized people in our cultures and societies;
—whatever promotes communities of men and women characterized by sharing and mutuality, joy and freedom;
—whatever respects and protects creation.

With the inconclusive discussion on hermeneutical principle and the disagreement over what it was for Asian women, it became obvious that some follow-up was needed. But this seemed a foregone conclusion even before the Seoul meeting took place. Aruna Gnanadason of India wrote to some Asian sisters a month before the Seoul consultation: "What I suggest is that we have a meeting of about 20-25 women . . . to put together some hermeneutical principles—a sort of collation of all our thoughts and ideas. I know that this is what is intended to happen in Seoul, but then two days will not be adequate . . . I suggest a five-day meeting."

Gnanadason's suggestion became a reality when a second consultation was organized to take place in Madras, India, from December 15 to 20, 1990, with Gnanadason as one of the coordinators. Building on the Seoul experience, the organizers[64] agreed that the two-fold purpose of the Madras meeting would be (1) to analyze the historical roots and development of patriarchy in different Asian nations, and the emergence of a feminist consciousness which challenges traditional attitudes and practices; and (2) to examine the evolving principles of feminist interpretation of events, scripture and theology arising from the new consciousness.

Preparations on the national level were set to meet this two-fold purpose. In addition, the national groups were asked that dialogue with the interpretive models of western feminist theologians as well as with male liberation theologians in their own country be part of their preparation. Based on the total findings, each national delegation was expected to produce a composite paper to be reported, critiqued, and refined in Madras.

The national groups used a variety of approaches to attain the desired goal. For example, the Philippine group discussed patriarchy with feminist historians and social scientists, and hermeneutics with both male and female liberation theologians before writing their composite paper. The Indian women met with their male EATWOT colleagues and compared similarities and differences in their theological endeavors, providing a notable contribution to the Madras meeting.

Not all the preparatory efforts ended satisfactorily, however. The Korean women, for instance, decided to focus on patriarchy in a series of sixteen seminars with young Marxist feminists, a significant move in light of the efforts towards the reunification of North and South Korea. Intended to enrich both groups, the seminars ended in frustration instead. Trying to combine opposing views on patriarchy and its development in Korea became a confusing and ineffectual exercise. As a result, the Korean delegation simply had to resign itself to presenting an unfinished paper at the consultation.

While not all arrived at the desired objective, on the whole the composite papers were done with much care and research. Some preferred to deal with other aspects in relation to hermeneutics. Sri Lanka, for one, treated the subject of "hermeneutical circle" instead.

What proved to be determining factors—whether helpful or limiting—in the search for an Asian women's hermeneutical principle were the country's history and culture, and the social, political, and economic contexts. In the case of Indonesia, for example, delving deep into their culture led the Indonesian women to see the interrelationship between men and women through *musyawarah* as an important element in their hermeneutical principle. *Musyawarah* can be described as genuine dialogue guided by inner wisdom leading to a communal decision within a community. Thus, through *musyawarah*, not only women but also men become committed in a cooperative venture to erasing the traces of patriarchy from the community. In Malaysia's case, on the other hand, the present political and religious climate deterred the women from making a serious analysis of the roots of patriarchy in the country [65] and coming up with a critical principle with which to interpret both text and context. In the Philippine situation, since virtually all precolonial records had been destroyed with the coming of Spain, the Filipino women had to call on feminist historians and anthropologists to "reconstruct" history in order to determine the roots of patriarchy prior to colonization. Because time prevented an adequate reconstruction, the Philippine group had to restrict its study to the type of western patriarchy introduced by Spain and which endures in the country to this day.

There was open and honest discussion after the presentation of each of the composite papers. What some essays missed, others supplied. While not explicitly stated in their own work, all the delegates agreed with the Hong Kong women's characterization of Asian feminist hermeneutics: that it should be grounded in the Asian religious and cultural contexts, and that it should reflect the struggles of Asian women for authentic womanhood. As expected, most of the papers expressed in similar ways what the Hong Kong report further stated on feminist hermeneutics:

> Since Asian women do not experience their indigenous religions and cultures in the same way as Asian men, their hermeneutical principles would be different from those of the male theologians. Furthermore, the struggles of Asian women are very different from the struggle of the white middle class women. Asian feminist theology should not be a replica of the white feminist discourse.[66]

It was not difficult to come to a common "statement" at the end of the consultation. While repeating much of what was said in the Seoul meeting, the Madras statement added what the women envisioned as the new society and what they perceived as the roots of patriarchy in Asia. The statement also made a clear distinction between Asian women's hermeneutical principles and Asian feminist methodology. The group agreed to express an Asian women's hermeneutical principle as an affirmation of:

—the full humanity of women in an authentic and inclusive community of peace, joy and freedom based on just relationships;
—the integrity of creation;
—the feminine creative principle as life-giving and life-enhancing;
—the prophetic and alternative voice and action of women in liberation movements; and
—the solidarity of women among ourselves and with others

supporting our struggles, as well as with people's movements.[67]

Gnanadason herself acknowledged in a post-consultation letter that while "we have not fully worked out hermeneutical principles, we see this as a first step." Nevertheless, the Madras consultation received a high rating from all the delegates. But the success of the meeting was due not so much to the quality of the essays as to the atmosphere of sisterhood and mutual respect that prevailed from the start as well as the bonding that grew as the women prayed, relaxed, discussed, and took meals together. Although the delegates went to the meeting to share the fruit of their research, they were also there to learn from one another and to recognize their common and diverse struggles as Asian women theologians. And this they did.

While satisfied with the Madras meeting, the Asian women know that theirs is still an unfinished work, an ongoing work that they need to do with each other's help. They look forward to being together again to chart their next course. But as part of the Women's Commission, they realize that theirs is not an isolated effort. Together with their EATWOT sisters from Africa and Latin America, their hope and task is to make their collective contribution an integral part of emerging Third World theologies.

# CHAPTER FIVE
◆ ◆ ◆

## EATWOT WOMEN:
## THEIR OWN THEOLOGICAL JOURNEYS

What has been recorded thus far is the development of the collective theological consciousness of EATWOT women. It has been gleaned from corporate activities and statements from 1976 to 1991. What is wanting for a more comprehensive picture is stories of individual women's theological journey. The stories would not only give flesh to the corporate accounts in the preceding pages but, in conjunction with those accounts, serve as basis for an analysis of the movement in the women's theological consciousness which will be accomplished in the following chapter. To gather the individual women's stories of their own theological journeys, I personally conducted interviews with eight EATWOT women from the Third World continents. Highlighted in the interviews were the origins and development of their theological consciousness, the commonalities and differences they perceived among EATWOT women, and what they saw as future tasks for themselves as Third World women theologians.[1]

The ecumenical nature of EATWOT was a determining factor in the selection of the interviewees.[2] At least one Catholic and one Protestant from each continent were selected. Those interviewed from Africa were Mercy Amba Oduyoye, a Ghanaian Methodist, and Teresa Okure, a Roman Catholic sister from Nigeria. From Latin America were Elsa Tamez, a Mexican Methodist now residing in Costa Rica, and Maria Clara Bingemer, a Brazilian lay Catholic. From Asia those interviewed were Mary John Mananzan, a Benedictine sister from the Philippines; Aruna Gnanadason, a member of the Church of South India; Kwok Pui-lan, an Anglican from Hong Kong; and Sun Ai Lee Park, Korean, who is an ordained minister of the Disciples of Christ.[3]

### African Women's Stories

*Mercy Amba Oduyoye*
Now deputy general secretary of the World Council of Churches in Geneva, Oduyoye was the first African woman to join EATWOT. Today's foremost African woman theologian, Oduyoye became involved in theology almost by accident. "It wasn't something I had thought through."[4] It was because "somebody thought I could study theology." This "somebody" was Prof. Noel King who was then trying to establish the Department of Divinity (later changed to Religious Studies) in the University of Ghana. Having taught for some years, Oduyoye had planned to do a certificate in Education at the university but was persuaded by Prof. King to take up the Divinity course instead.

By the time she graduated, Oduyoye was deep into theology and went for further studies at the University of Cambridge on a tutorial basis. As she went from origins of dogmas to doctrinal debates, from creeds to Christian rites in the Church, she found herself asking: What does all this have to do with the daily lives of people? After two years in Cambridge, she decided she had enough of academic theology and returned to Ghana to teach.

It was evident that Oduyoye's classes appreciated the way she correlated what was happening to people in the Bible and in Church history to what was happening to the people of Ghana. It dawned on Oduyoye that the theological studies she considered useless and irrelevant to life were really important to teaching religion to young people. "If you think they are irrelevant, it means you are not looking around you." Theology had to be correlated, accommodated, adapted to African life if it was to be relevant.

This insight was broadened and deepened as Oduyoye worked in the Youth Department, first of the WCC from 1967 to 1970 and later, of the All Africa Conference of Churches from 1970 to 1973. "In all these circles, you see how theology works in life, how theology relates to life." Having married the Nigerian theologian Modupe Oduyoye in 1968, Oduyoye moved to Nigeria at the end of her term in Geneva.

When she started teaching at the University of Ibadan, Oduyoye saw that the religion department there was "still teaching the kind of theology that I was running away from when I was in Cambridge." After much struggle, she was able to introduce a course in Contemporary Christian Theology, which was made up of liberation theology,

African theology, feminist theology, and the theological ferments in Britain in the 1960s and 1970s. Oduyoye found herself identifying with liberation theology and writers like Juan Luis Segundo. As she read Segundo's *The Liberation of Theology*,[5] she kept saying to herself, "That's it. We have to free theology from the traditional mode. This man is saying what I had been feeling and had been trying to say . . . Christian theology has not been free to address the African situation."

Oduyoye formally joined EATWOT in 1981 although she had been part of EATWOT activities since 1977, when Ghana became the site of the second EATWOT dialogue. When the irruption occurred in Delhi, she personally had no strong feeling that

> we must be heard or that men's perspective was wrong, but that there was another way of viewing situations that EATWOT was ignoring. For me it wasn't like a crusade. In fact, at that time I didn't specifically question the male language that we were using.[6]

In 1981, Oduyoye was offered the Dorothy Cadbury Fellowship at Selly Oaks Colleges in England. On one occasion she was asked to give a lecture on "The Doctrine of Man." In reading around the subject, she began to feel that "something was the matter . . . It looks like humanity was being defined by the male of the species. Man is the norm, and as a woman, I was not finding myself." When Oduyoye finally wrote the paper which she re-titled "Christian Anthropology," she said, "You cannot have a comprehensive, integrated Christian anthropology if you do not take into account a feminist perspective."[7]

After her Selly Oaks experience, Oduyoye started to react to public statements about African women, African culture, and African language. Though African women did not resonate with all aspects of the feminist movement in the West, Oduyoye would become impatient when men in international meetings would claim:

> African women are not oppressed . . . You look at the market women in western Africa. They are strong, they hold their own money, they run their own affairs. African women don't have any business joining any liberation movement because they are free.

To Oduyoye such claims sounded as if African women had never experienced oppression or colonization or Westernization.

It was the language issue that prompted Oduyoye to do her own research into feminism and into her own language and culture. Many things have been blamed on Western culture for promoting sexism, yet Oduyoye found socialization sayings in her own Akan language ripe with sexist allusions. Though the Akan are basically mother-centered, many of the folktales and proverbs are anti-women! Moreover, many Africans claim that they have always had mutuality. Oduyoye disagrees:

> The rituals around the rites of passage have not changed very much. They are ancient and they tilt in favor of men. The widowhood rites, for example. They say what you should do when the husband departs, but there are no equivalent rites that say what men should do when the wife departs. The dowry system is another example.[8]

While rites and rituals—Christian and African—with their effect on women remain a concern for Oduyoye and other African women, what she considers very important for her own theological reflection and where she has done her most creative writing is in the areas of Christian anthropology and the *imago Dei*, with their implications for community:

> I have worked out these themes very often. Human beings have to live in community and we don't know how to do it. African life is in a closely-knit community and we are always asking ourselves who is more important—me as a person or the community in which I live. The idea of the Holy Trinity as being united and yet diverse helped me very much.[9]

Despite her busy schedule at the WCC, Oduyoye makes time for EATWOT and its commissions. She sees the Women's Commission as having helped not only the EATWOT women but the men as well. Among EATWOT women, Oduyoye notes more commonalities than differences and sees them "moving in the same direction." However, though the Commission has helped to raise feminist consciousness, in Oduyoye's opinion it has not done very much on the language about God. "We very quickly brushed it aside as a Western issue. I think that if women in any part of the world are suffering, all other women should look into that suffering."

Oduyoye speaks proudly of the Circle[10] and of the Biennial

Institute of African Women in Religion and Culture, which she designed in 1989 on behalf of the African women of EATWOT. She envisions the final event of the project seven years hence as a celebration of the "end of the isolation and marginalization of African women in the study of these areas. It will also mark the beginning of the call for integration of these factors in deciding the direction of social change in Africa."[11]

### Teresa Okure

Like Oduyoye, Okure's initial interest was not in the study of theology. Okure received her primary and secondary education in eastern Nigeria. Having gone to high school with the Sisters of the Holy Child Jesus (SHCJ), she entered religious life after graduation, becoming the first African to join the congregation. As the Sisters had no formation house in Nigeria then, Okure was sent to their novitiate in England. In college Okure majored in English/French. It was not until 1976, when she was back in Nigeria and was named national program coordinator for the Sisters' Area Conference that Okure became interested in studying theology at the professional level.

> My frustration was setting up a program and not finding people to implement it . . . I discovered that we needed people highly trained theologically. My congregation had been thinking on-and-off whether I should begin theology or continue with French, which I was very good at. But the program and the need for personnel really got me interested.[12]

In 1977, Okure began graduate studies in theology at Fordham University. After receiving her M.A. in Scripture in 1979, she went on for her Ph.D. in the same university but spent two years at the Ecole Biblique in Jerusalem as part of her field work.

When Okure returned to Nigeria in 1985, she joined the Catholic Institute in West Africa (CIWA) as a professor in Scripture.

> It was a very different orientation from what I learned in Fordham, which was a very detached type of approach, "detached" in the sense of not being related to contemporary daily life issues. When I teach critical problems and methods in the Nigerian context, I have to ask myself: How relevant is all this? Does this methodological approach really help the interaction, the integration of Scriptures into the life of people?

Aware that Christianity had not really taken root in that part of Africa, the Associaiton of Episcopal Conferences of Anglophone West Africa (AECAWA) set up CIWA in 1981 to engage in a contextual approach to theology and Scripture. The African reality was to be a constitutive element in theological reflection and in biblical study and interpretation.

When Okure joined EATWOT in 1986, it was "like a shot in the arm, so to say." It served to consolidate the orientation of her thinking and that of CIWA. "It has helped me to help the Institute in what it is trying to do." Okure also attributes to EATWOT the incentive and imperative to go beyond contextualizing theology to doing theology by addressing specifically the issue of the African woman. She had been exposed to the feminist perspective while taking a course on women in the New Testament at Fordham, but it was not an entirely positive experience.[13] She tried reading some of the feminist writings, but ended up asking herself: What are they really looking for, what really is the issue? She ended up distancing herself instead. "I wasn't attracted to most of the things I read. For me they clouded the issue."

When she joined CIWA in 1985, one of the first things she was asked was to give a talk to African women on women's role in Church and society from a Scriptural perspective. "In a way, that was a transition, because I had to think of what would be helpful to them . . . and things like ritual did come up. But I was not really consciously thinking of a `Third World women's perspective' at that time." Even when Okure made her presentation on women in the Old Testament for the national consultation at Ibadan in 1985,[14] which she reworked for the Anglophone women's meeting in Port Harcourt and later for the intercontinental women's conference in Oaxtepec, she was not thinking in terms of "an African women's perspective."

It was in Oaxtepec that it really hit home. "The Latin American people were talking from a Latin American perspective, and the Asian women's approach was much more from their own context. Certainly my own paper wasn't from that." But while she saw the need for it, Okure confessed during the interview:

> I actually haven't gotten fully into that . . . I'm still dealing with—I don't want to say "universal"—basic principles before relating to concrete situations. I am still trying to see some basic principles which would call for a reinterpretation of Scripture, whether or not in the African

context or specifically from the women's perspective. I consider this approach very, very necessary.

Okure spoke of growth on her part since Oaxtepec. For the inaugural meeting of the Biennial Institute, she was asked to do a Bible study on Luke 8:40-56 which was on the raising of Jairus' daughter. [15] "You will see there a different orientation." Calling it her most representative work in this regard till the time of the interview, she wrote it with the theme of the consultation in mind: "Daughters of Africa, Arise!" Okure did it differently by first asking: How does this text speak to what we are to do at this consultation? For the first time, she felt she read formally, that is, in terms of publication, "the text from the African situation, specifically."

Okure's concern is not so much to speak or write from what scholars would regard as an African perspective as to get her male colleagues and students to discover that they have been conditioned by and fixed in one sole perspective in the interpretation of Scripture. Okure has since introduced a course on women in the New Testament in the all-male setting of CIWA. First given as a seminar outside the regular program, it is now a required subject. As a minimum, Okure aims at getting her students to see how Scripture has suffered for having been written, interpreted, and taught almost exclusively from a patriarchal perspective. The students have come to see "the injustice and inhumanity in what has been happening in the world with respect to women,"[16] an amazing phenomenon in a context where patriarchy is combined with clericalism.

To Okure, the pressing theological issues from an African women's perspective include not only the question of rituals and taboos which affect the women most, but also the subject of motherhood in terms that are person-centered. The African question in all theology is: What does all this have to do with life? Okure sees this as having a "natural affinity" to the kind of focus and emphasis that EATWOT women have. Serving as EATWOT's executive secretary at the time of the interview, Okure says that we EATWOT women

should not allow ourselves to become conditioned by the way the West has been theologizing. Our approach should be what is good for us. When you are personally involved, you see things differently. Growth takes time. What I mean is that we should not be expecting quick results but should make sure that there's real growth and orientation in the right direction.

### Latin American Women's Stories

*Maria Clara Bingemer*

Holder of a doctorate in theology from the Gregorian University in Rome, Bingemer is married and has three children. She was born and educated in Rio de Janeiro, and chose journalism as her major when she entered the university there. She then worked for the media department of the Brazilian Bishops' Conference. Part of her job consisted in producing audio-visuals for mass media, which demanded knowledge of content and not merely skills.

> I felt it would be good to study a little theology to deepen my knowledge of Christian doctrine. I began to study theology but without any intention of remaining in it. But I became more and more involved. Finally I left journalism and stayed in theology.[17]

In 1976, Bingemer enrolled in the Catholic University in Rio after a friend assured her that lay people—and not only priests or seminarians as she thought—could earn a theology degree there. At that time, Latin American liberation theology[18] was already taught in some schools, but it was not yet "consolidated." It had entered theological institutions more "as a hope." While some professors were already aware of, or themselves involved in, liberation theology, many were still repeating European theology. Thirteen years later, at the interview, Bingemer could say with assurance of liberation theology:

> It is taught in almost all the theological schools, at least the most serious ones. As a method of reflection, it has been assimilated to some extent even by those who don't share the vision of liberation theology.

Among Bingemer's professors was Joao Batista Libanio, a liberation theologian. Bingemer found herself "in sympathy" with the new model of theological reflection and began reading the published works in the early 1980s. It was also then that she met Leonardo Boff, who had been silenced by the Vatican and forbidden to write, publish, or teach theology. Boff asked her to substitute for him in his classes in Petropolis. She became more and more involved in liberation theology.

Being "involved" meant not just teaching in schools or seminaries. Since 1981, Bingemer's praxis has been with biblical circles [19] in a poor barrio in Rio. Bingemer also conducted formation classes for coordinators of such circles in one of the *favelas* (slums) of Rio. Putting her theological work at the service of the poor, she was often called upon to act as *asesora* [20] to groups in poor parishes and dioceses.

Although Bingemer was making significant contributions to liberation theology, she slowly became aware of missing perspectives. In her article, "Women in the Future of Liberation Theology," she specifies not only the perspective of women, but of blacks and Amerindians.

> These groups, oppressed for centuries by their color, race, and sex, are now essential for an evaluation of the theology of liberation and for any attempt to glimpse its future, because they bring to theology new issues, a new method, and a new language.[21]

Bingemer recounted how she first became conscious of theologizing from a Latin American woman's perspective. It was at the national meeting of women theologians in Brazil which she helped to organize in 1985 as part of the first phase of the Commission's five-year program. "That's when I began to be aware that doing theology as a woman—as a Latin American woman—was something special." This did not imply disregarding what men have done, or that just because it was done by men, it was not any good. Rather, women "have a special way of feeling things, of understanding things, of reflecting." Bingemer claims that Latin American men are idealistic in their vision of the feminine. Women, on the other hand, are realistic. "As a woman, you know what you are talking about because you live it, you experience it." Moreover, as women theologians we are called "to be attentive to what the women in the grass roots are suffering, thinking, and doing, and to make it part of theologizing."

Though not all the forty women who attended the national meeting were professional theologians, they all followed the line of liberation theology. When Bingemer was asked in the interview whether these women also followed the line of feminist theology, she answered affirmatively.

> Yes, but we understand feminist theology not in the same way as North American women understand it. At times it seems that North American feminism is an aggressive movement, a movement against someone or something. Ours in not a struggle

against, but a positive struggle, a struggle in favor of. We want men with us; we don't want to do anything against men.[22]

Bingemer felt that it was important for women's theological contribution to be taken seriously by male liberation theologians.

> It is a trap for us to deal only with the subject of women or feminism. We have to think, to write, and to teach about the big themes of theology: Christology, the Trinity, eschatology, and such. But we must stress that we do it as women.

Bingemer's first attempt at doing this was at the continental meeting in Buenos Aires in 1985, which was the second phase of the Commission's program. There she wrote an essay on the Trinity, which traced the "triple dualism" in theology and studied different "possible openings for a feminist Trinitarian theology." She saw in the Trinity "the ultimate possibility for integrating the masculine and the feminine."[23] For the Oaxtepec women's meeting in 1986, Bingemer wrote on Christology.[24]

In Oaxtepec, she noted differences in the way Third World women approached theology from a women's perspective, but what impressed her more were the similarities. One in particular stood out: doing theology from the perspective of women is "not an isolated job. It's a collective job. The theological subject is collective, not individualistic."[25] She saw the women being "very committed to one another," eager to share this "new awareness of being women" and to assert the necessity of solidarity.

Serving as Latin American coordinator for EATWOT at the time of the interview, Bingemer sees areas of concern that EATWOT women should examine together from the women's viewpoint. She singled out biblical hermeneutics, liturgy, and spirituality as needing women's distinctive gifts. Then she added what she said might be taken as an "audacious" suggestion:

> Women should work more on erotic themes: desire, pleasure, and the like. The Church has put away these themes from theological reflection, and it is important to rediscover all of them in healthy and open and deep ways... It is good to have the courage to begin.

Bingemer recognizes that the erotic, like the issue of ecology, is an issue not only for women but also for men, but she believes that women have a unique contribution to make to it because they "see the primacy of desire not only in doing theology but also in living the faith."

### Elsa Tamez

Tamez was brought up as a Presbyterian in Mexico. Born in 1950 into a poor family devoted to the Church, she grew up "close to religion, but in a romantic way."[26] Desiring "to help people and to preach Jesus Christ," Tamez at eighteen entered the Seminario Biblico Latinoamericano in Costa Rica.[27] It was there that she met her future husband and where she later joined the Methodist Church.

Towards the end of the 1960s, Central America was in a revolutionary situation, marked by struggles against repression, poverty, and oppression. Tamez began changing her "idealistic ideas about God and theology." The people's daily life and suffering were posing deep challenges to the churches and theology. Most of the seminary professors of the liberal line were then more concerned with secularism, but other professors began to introduce the incipient works of liberation theologians, such as Gutierrez and Rubem Alves, to the students.

Things started to connect for Tamez. While it was not so much the books as the repressive condition in Central America that prompted her to do theology in a liberating way, nevertheless, the works of the liberation theologians had a marked effect on her. "It was a great joy to read them because finally, there was a logical discourse that accompanied our concern." She saw the shortcomings of the "secular" theology. While secular theology spoke of "religion in the streets," it did not address the blatant reality of the poverty around them. It spoke of "man" in a generic way, but never specifically of the poor.

Like many Christians committed to the struggle for socioeconomic and political change, it was difficult for Tamez "to perceive other struggles when you see death very close to you. Peasants, workers, men, women, children, were dying every day." She saw the other specific struggles in a secondary way.

> I must confess that in the beginning I was not conscious of the oppression of women. You can see that in *Bible of the Oppressed,*[28] I wrote only one passage on women, about the violent oppression of the concubine which was so obvious. But little by little, I was challenged by other church women who said I must represent them.

Asked to write articles about women in journals, Tamez had to make an effort to read the Bible from a women's perspective.[29] Around this time, Tamez joined EATWOT. Looking back, she saw how her EATWOT membership had helped her.

> The Delhi experience was very important for me. If you remember I wrote that biblical reflection on Hagar, and I saw Hagar as triply oppressed—as slave, as woman, and as Egyptian.[30]

While the idea for her two books of interviews with liberation theologians came from her experience in EATWOT, it was liberation theology that facilitated her developing a feminist consciousness, "because its starting point is oppression." She quickly added, "But we have to say it's not only economic oppression. Black people are also among the excluded as well as women. Liberation theologians have to realize that this method has to include all kinds of oppression."

At the time of the interview, Tamez was working on her thesis for a doctorate in theology at the University of Lausanne in Switzerland. She explained why she chose the theme of "justification by faith."[31]

> The problem in Latin America and in the Third World is that women have to struggle on many fronts. We have to have present before us all the issues, such as women's issues, poverty, racism, other religions. And then we also have to struggle against classical theology."

She explained that "justification by faith" in classical theology has been very deeply internalized by the Protestants in Latin America. Moreover, "liberation theologians are criticized that we don't take grace seriously, only praxis. So my concern is how to read this passage from a liberation perspective."[32] Tamez continued unapologetically, "At this moment you can say that my thesis represents my latest theological thinking as a Latin American woman."

Latin American women are still searching for the way to express theology so that it incorporates the women's point of view.

> It is easy for us to say how to do it, but in the actual implementation it is not that easy. There's the problem of different approaches and theories; there's no consen-sus. All we are sure of is that there is an oppression beyond the economic that has to do with one's sex.

Tamez opined that in many cases, Latin American women first accepted liberation theology before acquiring a women's perspective, and that this was true even of women in the popular movements, not only in theology. Tamez felt that the option for the poor that is strong in Latin America was something that all EATWOT women had in common.

For Tamez it is important for EATWOT women to continue working on projects together.

> I think that women have made an important contribution to biblical hermeneutics. Now it seems that it would be good for us to start working on some of the classical themes in theology, like ecclesiology, soteriology, pneumatology, and the very question of what is theology. Perhaps it is not right to continue with these themes from Western theology, but somehow I think women should try to rework those major doctrinal themes from history that we learned in the seminary.

To Tamez's mind, these were part of EATWOT women's pending tasks. "We cannot take it for granted that we have really grasped what it means to do theology from a women's perspective. We should look at existing feminist theories and critique them from a Third World perspective. Our analysis of women's situation should be as serious and as scientific as our analysis of economic oppression."

### Asian Women's Stories

#### Mary John Mananzan

Mananzan was born in 1937 of a middle class family. Educated by Benedictine Sisters through college, it was not a surprise when she joined the congregation after receiving an A.B. in History from St. Scholastica's College. While she became interested in theology after she became a sister, when she was sent to Germany for post-graduate studies, she chose philosophy instead. "A Ph.D. in theology meant spending three years in classical languages which I would not be using anyway."[33] She majored in linguistic analysis and had two minors: systematic theology and missiology.

After six years of studies Mananzan returned to Manila in 1973, a year after martial law was declared in the Philippines. While teaching contemporary philosophy at a Jesuit university, she joined the Interfaith Theological Circle which aimed at contextualizing theology. The members put together reflections on what was happening under the one-man rule of Ferdinand Marcos, but they were severely criticized by people in the liberation movement for doing this in the university's air-conditioned library. It was not long before Mananzan herself realized "it was indeed futile to evolve such a theology without getting involved in the struggle of the people."[34]

Mananzan's first involvement was with striking workers, which also immersed her in the problems of slum dwellers. The deeper she became involved with the struggling poor, the clearer she saw the need for raising church people's consciousness and for doing theology from the people's perspective. It was not a matter of applying revelation or doctrine to people's lives, but starting with people's lives and experience and seeing their meaning in the light of faith. Thus, concurrent with her involvement in people's movements, Mananzan became active in helping church-related groups to analyze and reflect on the present Philippine reality from a liberational perspective.[35]

Mananzan admitted that her association with EATWOT since the early 1980s helped her to deepen this liberational thrust and to see the new theological method as an integral process. It was also as an EATWOT member that she began to theologize from a women's perspective.

This started in Geneva in 1983 when she was helping to formulate the proposal for a women's commission. There Mananzan became fully conscious of the need for the women's perspective in any liberational theology. By that time she had been active in women's organizations. She herself had helped to found several women's groups. She was one of the co-founders of Pilipina in 1978, "which can be considered the first organization of women with a conscious and expressed feminist orientation"[36] in the Philippines. In 1979, she co-founded the Center for Women's Resources. But for Mananzan, being involved in women's issues and theologizing were two separate activities. Somehow, "they did not yet merge. I did not have the idea of analyzing gender issues in theology."

What further helped Mananzan develop gender consciousness in theologizing was her appointment as EATWOT program coordinator in 1985. "As I followed step by step what we did in the national meetings, but more especially in the Asian consultation in 1985, I became more conscious of beginning with our experience of oppression and our own struggle as women." The consultation also brought home the necessity of cultural critique, often passed over lightly by male liberation theologians, and the collective nature of feminist theologizing.

For the Asian consultation in 1985, Mananzan wrote an article on the emerging spirituality of Asian women,[37] which, together with "Theological Perspectives,"[38] she considered her most representative works at the time of the interview. "I am now very gender conscious in the articles I write and in the talks I give. When I wrote recently on the impact of Vatican II on Southeast Asia, I made a particular critique of its lack of a women's perspective."

When the office of program coordinator was suspended by the next set of EATWOT officers, Mananzan felt that something was lost in "the forward thrust" of the Women's Commission. Without a common focus, the Commission could not advance as a group.[39] "For instance, we are searching for our hermeneutical principle as Asian women, but we don't know what they are doing in Africa or in Latin America." It was Mananzan's opinion that Third World women could have common hermeneutical principles, different from those of the West. "There is a difference between oppressor countries and oppressed countries . . . but oppressed countries can have the same hermeneutical principle." Mananzan acknowledged there would be nuances.

With common hermeneutical principles, Mananzan saw re-working the major theological themes as a common agenda for the Women's Commission. "We have to tackle Christology, ecclesiology, anthropology, missiology, from the perspective of women." She felt that the Commission should provide the venue for this. She added that serious theological reflec-tion in the Third World was still needed on such pressing issues as violence against women, battering, rape, incest. "We are always talking about method, about what it means to be a feminist theologian of liberation. If we have this agenda, then let's go about it!"

### Aruna Gnanadason

It was only in 1986 that Indian women became EATWOT members. Among them was Gnanadason, presently the director of the WCC sub-unit on Women in Church and Society.

Gnanadason's faith foundation was laid in early childhood. Her grandmother insisted on Christian education, daily Bible reading, and going to Church twice on Sundays. This rigidity had an opposite effect on Gnanadason. When her grandmother died, she stopped going to church. "I rejected the whole thing."[40] Even when she joined the Christian Student Movement with its strong stress on the social message of the gospel, she remained critical of the practices her grandmother taught her.

Gnanadason's first job was in the Ecumenical Christian Center (ECC) in Bangalore, with sociopolitical analysis as her specialization. Having a strong Marxist orientation, Gnanadason was then very critical of feminists, giving the usual arguments of how they were dividing the working class. It was not long before the lower and middle class women in ECC became critical of Gnanadason in return, claiming that her analysis failed to take into consideration the experience of women. Listening to the women's stories, Gnanadason realized her own oppression as a woman for the first time. "It was a real transformation I went through." She joined the secular women's movement shortly after and began analyzing the situation of Indian women. "I discovered this system of patriarchy and my whole analysis changed. I realized how inadequate my Marxist analysis had been."

Gnanadason became a committed feminist, but "still my Christianity was divorced from all this. I didn't see the need to delve into Christianity for anything." It was about this time that she had her first contact with EATWOT. Gnanadason recalled how a number of the top male liberation theologians of India were meeting at the ECC to prepare for an EATWOT conference. She was asked to join them because they needed a female presence. "It was a horrifying experience for two days. I just sat there like a zombie with nothing to say. Yet all the time I was conscious that something was missing."

As Gnanadason's feminist consciousness grew, she became more and more disaffected with the ECC which was not used to dealing with women's issues in this new way. When she was offered an opportunity to work with church women, she grabbed the chance, not because of her faith in church women but because she needed the job. "I was pretty arrogant about the fact that they had no consciousness of the women's movement or the issues they should be dealing with."

The eight years with the All India Council of Christian Women proved to be "the most creative years of my life." Gnanadason admitted that "working with churchwomen brought me back to my faith." Gnanadason began reading the Bible with new eyes, and that spurred an interest in theology. If she was to reach Christian women, she had to do everything to empower them. It was with this resolve in mind that she jumped at the offer from the EATWOT Women's Commission to help organize a national meeting on theology in 1984.[41] "From then on, there was no turning back."

Gnanadason was impressed with the books by feminists from the West which she had started reading. *"In Memory of Her*[42] and *Sexism and God-talk*[43] were the cause of a conversion experience for me. I realized what the women in India were missing by not reading the Bible from a feminist perspective." She was inspired by the feminist theologians who had "the courage to critique traditional theology in such a scholarly way" and whose works were "getting accepted in theological circles as a valid new perspective."

Gnanadason sustained her relationship with secular women's groups at the same time, but Gnanadason noted a big shift in her thinking:

> from consciousness of just women's issues to a recognition of the feminist paradigm as a new political vision. Women have to go beyond being victims into providing political alternatives. If we're going to critique the traditional male theology we've inherited, then we have to provide a new alternative vision. The alternatives we have so far are inadequate as they ignore the experience of women and other oppressed groups.

Gnanadason became keen on having Indian women develop hermeneutical principles which would take seriously both the Indian context and the Indian heritage. She was continually making new discoveries about her own cultural tradition. In her study of nature symbols in India, for example, she discovered they were all feminine and fertility-oriented or related to the creativity of the earth. Although she was prompted to do this study more out of her consciousness of ecology than her feminist consciousness, she saw "how crucial it was for feminist theologians in India to rediscover the feminist symbols and reclaim much of this heritage we have lost. We can draw a lot of power from that."

EATWOT had an important role to play in the growth of Gnanadason's theological consciousness. First, it was a break-through to work with Catholic women. "Protestant women were nervous about this, saying we're theologically different." But when they held the national meeting in 1984, Gnanadason saw no divisions between the Catholic, Protestant, and Orthodox women, and "since then we have worked together and stayed together." Second, her analysis has deepened. Her own understanding of patriarchy as an overarching reality and of the perspective of other Asian women developed in EATWOT. "I owe a lot to EATWOT. I've been very empowered."

Two years ago, Gnanadason began formal studies in theology. "I had repeatedly rebelled against it, trying to tell the world I didn't need theological education." Reading the works of feminist theologians, Gnanadason became convinced she "needed to know more about what traditional theology is saying." She finally registered for a Bachelor of Divinity. For Gnanadason, taking formal studies in theology is ironic after "I've given talks on feminist theology in all the major theological colleges in India, including the college where I'm now registered." She has had one dismaying experience: none of her reading lists so far has the name of a woman!

Her own dream for EATWOT women is that someday they would "be read just like Ruether and Schussler Fiorenza are read by women all over the world." However, she cautions that "we could be swept off our feet by Western feminist theologians. We have to be grounded in our own context and in the lives of our own women. We have to keep our roots strong."

### Kwok Pui-lan

Kwok's parents, originally farmers in China, went as refugees to Hong Kong soon after World War II. There Kwok was born in 1952 and grew up sometimes without the basic necessities. Hers was a typical patriarchal Chinese family with the need to have male children. Her mother bore five daughters before two sons finally came. "As the third child I was often dressed as a boy, so I grew up as a tomboy, trying to step out of the bounds of what a girl's life should be."[44] Kwok recalled:

> Growing up in that kind of life, I had some sort of feminist consciousness even when I was young, but I did not know the word. I grew up always questioning why it was always the boys who got the attention and the benefits and not the daughters.

Kwok became rebellious against her own patriarchal family for not being just, as well as against the whole system of socialization.

At the age of twelve, Kwok came in contact with the Anglican Church in Hong Kong which she later joined. The Church gave her another sphere, another space in which to move around and to have fellowship with other people, and it quickly became her second home. It was there that she met Huang Xianyun, then a deacon and later officially ordained as one of the first two women priests in the Anglican Communion.[45] Rev. Huang became a role model for Kwok. When Kwok decided to enter the seminary to study theology, she received her greatest encouragement from her.

A talk by a seminary professor convinced Kwok "there was so much more to Christian faith than Sunday school jargons." When she talked to her bishop about entering the seminary, she made it clear she was doing so "not so much for ordination, but because of a burning desire to know more about my faith."

In the course of her studies in the 1970s, Kwok had questions about the women's perspective in theology, but she was frustrated, not having a single woman professor in the whole school to provide answers. The first help came from an ethics teacher from Canada who introduced to her the works of Mary Daly and Rosemary Ruether. "It dawned on me there were people trying to articulate theology from a women's perspective. This was very important for me."

Another boost came from the students' movement. "We started study groups on Marxism and contemporary China. We paid a lot of attention to women's issues . . . making comparisons and trying to analyze and understand what happened to Chinese women given the socialist revolution."

Since her seminary days, Kwok had been involved in the ecumenical movement in Asia and was present when the CCA was inaugurated in 1973. In ecumenical gatherings, she became more aware of the reality of the sufferings of Asian women.

Kwok taught for two years after graduation. She later had an offer from her seminary to go on for further studies. She chose the field of ethics, doing her main research on the issues of justice and power. She wanted to relate these to the Chinese situation, but then "I didn't focus too much on the women's or feminist issue in China."

After receiving her M.Th., Kwok became the first woman professor at the seminary. Offering a course on "Women and the Church," she discussed the works of U.S. feminist theologians such as Daly, Ruether, and Russell. "At that time we needed to work with Western sources. In 1979, Katoppo's work was published, but there were very few resources on feminist theology from an Asian perspective." Nevertheless, for Kwok it was like sowing seeds. Some of her students later formed the Hong Kong Women Christian Council.

In 1984, Kwok began her doctoral studies at Harvard University.

Boston turned out to be a very important city for feminist studies. Not only were there important Christian feminist theologians but also Jewish feminist theologians and scholars from other faiths. There were also those into Goddess worship. The Christian feminists were struggling within the wider feminist movement trying to defend their faith against the critique of others who say that one cannot be a Christian and a feminist. There were a lot of different perspectives.

It was exciting for Kwok to share some of the insights and methodological viewpoints of feminist theologians in the United States. "They had to rediscover the roots of patriarchy as well as the liberating aspects of the Bible." Schussler Fiorenza's theological reconstruction of Christian origins was also inspiring because it offers important methodological clues. While studying in the United States, Kwok had the chance to meet Oduyoye, Tamez, and Afro-American theologians, such as Katie Geneva Cannon and Delores Williams, whose works encouraged Kwok to search for her own heritage as a Chinese woman.

For Kwok the history of Christianity in one's own particular context is important for women to grapple with. For example, from the Chinese viewpoint, Christianity was not looked upon as "a religion from the underside" but as "the religion of the imperialists." Failing to attract the rich and the literati, Protestant missionaries worked with common village folks and formed Christian communities among the lower class. For Chinese women, Kwok said:

Christianity was not seen as such an oppressive force. The Christian churches provided space for women to build peer bonding and to work in ways not possible in Chinese society in those days. There must have been something in Christianity that they found helpful, because many women joined the Church despite many persecutions.

Kwok later reflected in an article she wrote:

To claim such a heritage for myself is a process of self-empowerment. First, it informs me that these Chinese Christian women have a history and a story that need to be recovered for the benefit of the whole church . . . It is because of this history that I can claim to do theology from a Chinese woman's perspective.[46]

What was helpful to Kwok was the Christian symbolisms which women transformed and adapted in the Chinese tradition. Recalling her own process, she concluded:

> You need to engage in dialogue with your foremothers and learn some of the things they have reached. People think they are not important, but making the connection helps to build your own church history from the women's point of view.

Kwok thinks that the Asian EATWOT women's regional project should include a more serious critique of patriarchy. Unlike their sisters in Europe and North America as well as in Africa and Latin America, Asians must deal with the relationship between Asian religions and patriarchy. All this work should lead to new hermeneutical models when looking at theology and the Bible. This is in fact part of Kwok's special interest—to understand the Bible from the point of view of a "non-biblical world."[47]

As a participant in the Madras meeting of EATWOT women, she noted that the topic of family came up very frequently, but there was an "ambivalent analysis of women's role in the family, so this whole area of women and family should be elaborated." She also noticed that while all agreed that "as Asians we are communal, communitarian," there was no discussion on the question of women's self-identity—the self as an individual within a communitarian society—or on the aspects of community which truly liberate and on those which do not.

Asian women need to encourage and help each other "to develop our own theology, making use of people's stories, myths, poems, and lullabies . . . of new symbols and images to evoke fresh thinking." For Kwok, theology should not be a dry discourse but an art which touches people's hearts.

### Sun Ai Lee Park

Lee Park was born in Pyongyang, North Korea. She recalls that in her family, church life was "very, very important." Big events in the church, like Christmas, were celebrated not only with a big dinner but with worship and songs. Taking Christianity seriously as a teenager, she often asked questions about the meaning of life and about the Creator God of the universe, but she never got satisfactory answers.

As a student in a co-ed university, Lee Park was part of a small group of young men and women who gathered together each day for a prayer session. "It was a real community. We read the Bible and just talked among ourselves about life and about the country, without using any commentaries."[48] Still, Lee Park did not think of herself as going into theology. "Maybe I had a cultural bias. I thought of theology as something the menfolk did. It was not an attractive field for me." Instead, she went into Korean literature, finding the literary expressions in poems and novels more appealing. When later she received a scholarship to study theology in the United States, she chose to go into religious education and not into theology per se.

During her studies in the United States, she met her future husband, Sang Jung Park, and returned to Korea with him. "Since then, my life journey has been closely linked with my husband's life." When her husband was asked to be a staff person at the WCC, Lee Park left her job as assistant to the director of the language institute at Yonsei University and went with her husband to Geneva.

Lee Park's life in Geneva was that of a "typical middle-class housewife." Becoming active in an "ecumenical wives'" group, she was invited to the first world conference for women in Berlin in 1974.[49] She had mixed reactions about the conference. At times she felt that "the women were going too far," and yet it was at that conference that her world view was expanded. "Until then I was not conscious of women's issues." After her Berlin experience, she became convinced she "really had to do some theological studies."

This opportunity came when her husband was invited to teach in Emory University in Atlanta, Georgia. At first diffident about being a student again, she began by auditing a class and gained enough confidence to ask for a tuition scholarship. In two years, she received her master's degree in Divinity. "I wrote my dissertation on a comparison between Jurgen Moltmann and Kim Chi Ha . . . There was no feminist theology offered then."

During this time Lee park gradually became aware of the sexism of Korean men. "There were these Korean men working for democracy and human rights in Korea. They said they want democracy in the country, but when it came to women, it was something else! I started wondering what kind of democracy they were looking for." With the experience of sexism from her own Korean male colleagues, it dawned on her "why all the complaints and the cry against sexism in West Berlin!"

Lee Park could not remember how she started reading feminist theology. "It was fascinating . . . I read Russell and Ruether and their writings really made sense to me." That was the beginning for Lee Park. Then she was introduced to EATWOT when one of the Korean women could not attend the Delhi conference and needed a substitute. She remembered that the Third World theology in Delhi was still very much male-centered; however, she also recalled that there "you were already talking about the dialogue between First and Third World theologians . . . and you said there were going to be many Western feminist theologians." She knew then that she wanted to go.

In the meantime, Lee Park's husband had been elected general secretary of the Christian Conference of Asia and the family moved to Singapore. This turned out to be a creative period in Lee Park's life. She no longer wanted to be just an "ecumenical wife." Uprooted from her own country with no job provision in the host country, Lee Park decided "not to be wasted but instead do something for the concerns of Asian women doing theology."[50] In 1982, through her initiative, *In God's Image* was born, the only women's journal in Asia through which Asian women can share their theological thoughts—their reality, struggles, faith reflections, and aspirations for change.[51] It was also during this period that Lee Park founded the Asian Women's Resource Centre for Culture and Theology.

Lee Park was pleased when the EATWOT women's program was formulated in Geneva in 1983 and became its Asian coordinator. While EATWOT has helped her with social analysis and general methodology, it was through the Women's Commission that she was able to combine social context and women's perspective. "Now whatever I write, I try to include these two aspects." As an example, she spoke of her article, "Envisioning a Future Church as an Asian Woman,"[52] which she wrote for the multi-cultural program on feminist theology held in Maryknoll, New York, in the summer of 1989. After describing the patriarchal reality in Asia and its effects on women, Lee Park wrote, "The future church cannot be envisioned without taking into consideration the present social context" (p. 6). Thus the future church should not only be modeled after the Jesus community which was open to the contribution of women and other people who were discriminated against, but be freed from sexism, stand with the people's movement, and be a bearer of justice and a peace church (see pp. 6-16).

Having spent much time in the United States, Lee Park has a better understanding of Western feminism and feminist theology than most Asian women. "Feminist theology has many different trends; we cannot lump them all in one basket. There are those who think of feminism as an independent issue and those who try to make connections with other oppressions." She admits having been greatly inspired by Western feminist theologians and takes exception to having their influence on other Asian women minimized. But she adds, "We have to establish our own contextual theology, but I think we can dialogue with Western feminist theology, especially in the area of theory."

> If their theories are inadequate, we must prove so. On the other hand, everybody in Asia reads their writings regardless of the talk of indigenization, etc. I don't think we should pretend they don't exist or have no valuable contribution to make for us. I think at this stage critical evaluation is necessary.[53]

She believes that Third World women "can't afford to talk of women's issues alone." Most Korean women, for example, start from justice issues, problems of human rights, or the struggle for reunification or democratization. Though they themselves experience sexism, they make the interconnection not on the basis of sexism but of social injustice.

For Asian EATWOT women, Lee Park sees more work needed on interfaith dialogue from women's perspective as well as on hermeneutical principles and methodologies. "Methods are value-free neutral things, but our principle should be liberational. We have to go beyond experience and apply academic approaches as a next stage." As in Bible studies, academic research should not be left out of formulating principles. On the practical level, Lee Park would like to see more women's organizations coming together to organize conferences and to deepen their sisterhood.

## Comparing the Women's Journeys

As each woman shared her theological journey, similarities and differences came through in the way the journeys began and developed. How are these related to the similarities and differences that surfaced in the course of the EATWOT women's corporate journey? What is the relevance of the individual journeys to the collective effort towards more relevant and inclusive Third World theologies? These questions will form the basis of the analysis in the next chapter.

# CHAPTER SIX
◆ ◆ ◆

## EATWOT WOMEN EN ROUTE

During the interview with Oduyoye, she said this about EATWOT women:

> Whether we like it or not, we are rather a select group of women theologians. All of us are trying to ensure that theology becomes a liberating enterprise. In Oaxtepec I saw that we were moving in the same direction.[1]

That there are many similarities among EATWOT women is understandable and even to be expected. As EATWOT members, we accept the Association's liberation orientation, its theological assumptions, and general methodology.[2] This means doing theology from below and placing it at the service of the poor and oppressed who are struggling for full humanity. As part of the Women's Commission, we further commit ourselves to promote an inclusive Third World theology that takes women's being, viewpoint, and experience seriously. As Third World women, we are confronted with the experience of multiple oppression that besets all Third World women. As Oduyoye further observed, "When we look at the social situation of women, their economic situation, their situation in the Church . . . we tend to talk about the same things." It is no wonder that regarding the women's conference in Oaxtepec, with its common program, goal, and guidelines, Tamez could remark: "When we meet together as women, it is harder to see the differences and easier to see the similarities."

Yet in Oaxtepec, differences surfaced as recorded in the final document.[3] And indeed, after Oaxtepec, no longer bound by a common program with an over-all coordinator, the EATWOT women on the three continents did not "move in the same direction" but chose divergent trajectories.

In this chapter, first I shall propose an analysis of the similarities and differences in the development of the EATWOT women's theological consciousness. Then I will offer a critique and assessment of three aspects of that development: (1) the influence of context; (2) the function of methodology; and (3) the role of EATWOT.

### Different but Similar

The previous chapters traced the origins and growth of EATWOT women's theological consciousness on two levels: on the corporate level based on EATWOT events and documents, and on the individual level based on the stories of eight members. Though the women represent three continents and reflect different cultures, a clear progression can be traced on the corporate level as demonstrated in the study of three major EATWOT events: in New Delhi in 1981, in Geneva in 1983, and in Oaxtepec in 1986.

Before these events, EATWOT members, women and men alike, were engaged in developing contextual theologies that addressed their Third World situation of injustice and oppression. Their conference statements denounced all forms of oppression as part of the effort toward a more just and egalitarian society. In New Delhi, however, the experience of the "irruption"[4] awakened the women to the fact that despite EATWOT's liberative thrust and statements on women's equality, theologizing in EATWOT was in fact male-dominated and male-oriented. The women realized they had to create their own space within EATWOT to ensure that their voice would be included in the liberative Third World theologies EATWOT was promoting.

In the EATWOT dialogue with First World theologians in Geneva, it became clearer to the women that to make their theological contribution precisely as Third World women, they had to define their own agenda, separate from that of Third World male theologians as well as from First World feminists. In Geneva, the "space" took the shape of a women's commission within EATWOT, with a common program for the three continents. Thus began the women's conscious and collective effort to do theology from the perspective of Third World women to ensure that Third World theology would become truly liberating and inclusive in its mode and content.

In Oaxtepec in 1986, as EATWOT women gathered to share their experience of the previous three years, they found that, while holding some views in common, they had something different from their Third World brothers and First World sisters to say, and even from one another. While they saw that their theology had the common goal of liberation for all, they also observed divergences in their approach and emphases, and acknowledged the critical role of context in determining theological questions and priorities. They recognized that their faith demanded "total rupture with the prevailing patriarchal system"; at the same time, compassion and solidarity were singled out as necessary components in their methodology. At the ensuing EATWOT assembly in Oaxtepec, they saw a double task ahead of them: to supply missing content, true, but also to change the whole style of doing theology.

These three events reveal a gradual growth in the EATWOT women's corporate consciousness[5] from a limited liberational viewpoint to a more inclusive women's liberational perspective in their effort to contextualize theology. The women realized that their theology must include a broader methodological framework which incorporates a critical understanding of women's oppressive situation in their particular context and an active commitment to transform it.[6]

### Similar but Different

The individual accounts do not reveal any single pattern of development. But in most of the accounts, there was noticeable congruence with the corporate pattern of the women's development. The stories reveal that most of the women interviewed began their theological involvement without any clear women's consciousness and without any special focus on women. This is borne out, for example, in the stories shared by Oduyoye, Mananzan, and Tamez. After years of academic training, Oduyoye realized that for theology to be meaningful in Africa, it had to relate to the daily life and aspirations of the African people, not necessarily with a focus on women. In a parallel manner, Mananzan saw that the theology she had studied in Europe failed to address the repressive situation in her country during the years of martial law. If theology was to be relevant to the Filipino people, it had to take the people's struggle for justice and liberation seriously. Similarly, Tamez found that the liberal "secular" theology she was taught had no word for the dire poverty in Latin America, and it was liberation theology that addressed this major concern in terms of engagement and reflection. Thus whether the approach was more cultural (Oduyoye) or political (Mananzan), or economic (Tamez), they all came to the same conclusion that theology must be liberating for their people.

It was only after the Delhi incident that these women became aware that the liberation theology they were promoting lacked an important perspective—their own as Third World women—and they began supplying it. This pattern of growth in the women's theological consciousness is not surprising in terms of the women who became part of the EATWOT network prior to the formation of the Women's Commission in 1983.[7] Though they were aware of gender discrimination and were exposed to Western feminist literature, their main involvement was in the struggle they shared with their brothers against unjust structures, systems, and institutions, toward a more human life for all. They were concerned with the general survival and the daily struggles of their people—political, economic, and cultural. In their Third World situation where the scars of colonialism and the heavy burden of neocolonialism loomed large, the specific issue of gender oppression remained in the background[8]  In such a situation, it was easier to recognize and reject the *Western*, rather than the *male*, trappings of theology.

The individual stories reveal, however, that not all EATWOT women followed the corporate path in their own theological journey. Kwok's journey, for example, is a case in point. Early on, she became aware of the patriarchal practices in her home and in her church, and was already conscious of a women's perspective at the start of her studies and career in theology. Furthermore, Kwok pointed out that "liberation theology" did not have much attraction for a people who had no "liberational" alternatives. It was a matter of being ruled by Britain or the People's Republic of China, and Hong Kong people were aware of the excesses of the socialist regime so close to them, especially at the time of the Cultural Revolution. "Our first encounter with liberation theology was from Latin America. You can see why many of us in Hong Kong resisted this kind of theology that used Marxist analysis as part of its methodology."[9]

Whether or not the women followed a specific pattern of growth, what emerges from this analysis is the influence of context on the development of theological consciousness. In collective theologizing such as that done by EATWOT women, how the concrete context is *read*—what is considered life-threatening and what is seen as life-preserving within their reality—determines to a large extent the direction they take in their theological involvement.

## The Influence of Context

### The Choice of Priorities

The influence of context is more observable in the tasks the EATWOT women of each continent adopted for themselves in the post-Oaxtepec period. In Africa, where woman is oppressed by culture and religion no matter where she stands on the continent, the EATWOT women chose religious rites, cultural attitudes and practices as the focus of their study and action. This means examining seriously those customs and practices in the culture which are imposed on women because they are born female and which reinforce their subjugated status. Rites and rituals are an important part of African life, so it is a not just a matter of eliminating those that further their degradation, but of creating new ones or transforming those that would enhance women's lives.[10]

In contrast, religious rites and taboos surrounding females are not a concern for Latin American women. Their writings, as well as conversations with them in Oaxtepec, reveal that only recently have a few of them begun to explore Afro-Brazilian cults and traditions in connection with women's religious experience. Moreover, in Latin America, the focus is more on how these cults empower women rather than on how they subjugate them.[11]

Already scarred by poverty and oppression, Latin America is further marked by macho ideology. Because of this particular situation, the Latin American women have taken pains to address the adverse effects of this male-favoring ideology on church and society, and to stress the urgent need to include women's perspective in liberation theology. As Latin American women theologize within the framework of liberation theology, they favor reworking the same traditional theological themes[12] as their male colleagues, but from a woman's "optic."

By contrast, African and Asian women prefer to work independently of any prevailing Third World theology on their continents, no matter how liberational it may be.[13] In Asia, one group of Korean women theologians have begun developing a "minjung women's theology" which they claim is not out of the framework of minjung theology. One of them explains their effort as follows: "We cannot say we have the same framework and that we are just bringing in the women's perspective. The insights of minjung theology and the insights of the women's theology must meet, but together it will mean a new, more inclusive framework."[14] In Africa, the women have been cautious toward the efforts of male theologians to inculturate theology since they believe the men tend "to falsify cultural developments in Africa as these affect women and peasants."[15] Furthermore, the all-male theologians of "anthropological poverty" do not seem "aware of the cultural factors that marginalize and silence women."[16]

While sharing some of the concerns of their African and Latin American sisters, Asian women chose a different focus in the post-Oaxtepec years. As Asians they have a rich religious heritage; at the same time they are aware that Asian religions have been the source of immeasurable suffering for women due to patriarchal beliefs and practices. To arrive at a theology that is emancipating for Asian women—whether they are Christian or not—it became expedient to dig into the roots of patriarchy on the continent and at the same time uncover the liberating aspects in their cultural and religious heritage, in order to arrive at hermeneutical principles for interpreting texts and events. In comparison, African women do not consider taking time to study patriarchy as urgent or necessary. Faced daily with pressing issues such as problems in the economy which affect their existence, militarism, racism, and the refugee situation, they see the search for a conceptual frame of patriarchy as remote and insignificant.[17]

### The Content of Theology

The present study shows that context influences not only the focus of the women's theological tasks but the content of their reflections as well. A good example of this is seen in the EATWOT women's attempt to reformulate Christology from a Third World women's perspective. While EATWOT women see Christology as central to their theology and hold many views in common, their claims and emphases show the marked conditioning of context.[18] In Africa where women are subjected to demeaning customs[19] and are often led to think of themselves as "nobody" or "nothing,"[20] African women see a Jesus who is in affinity with their suffering, who seeks their empowerment, and encourages their self-affirmation. Jesus is seen as healer and nurturer, teacher and friend, who opposed the oppressive religious and cultural practices of his day. For them, Jesus of Nazareth is "uniquely the Christ of God," the "God in human image," whose life and praxis bear the message of liberation for all. [21]

In Latin America, a largely Christian continent where the struggle of the poor against economic and political domination gave birth to liberation theology, the hope of a new social order remains against great odds. Because women need liberation from both gender and politico-economic oppression, Christology for the Latin American women takes on the hues of a liberation Christology, but done from a women's perspective. Together with male liberation theologians, Latin American women hold the christological affirmations that "Jesus is God," "Jesus is the Christ," and "the Christ is Jesus." But Latin American women expose and reject the patriarchalization of Christology throughout history as well as the dichotomization between the "historical Jesus" and the "risen Christ," which has distorted Christology and has put women's humanity and their salvation "in the shadow for so long." [22]

In contrast to Latin America, Asia is a vast and complex continent that is less than three percent Christian. Thus most of Asia's women are adherents of other religious traditions; at the same time, they form the majority of Asia's poor and oppressed. In such a milieu, EATWOT women in Asia seek a Christology that is liberating for women while respectful of religious pluralism as well. Hence while they value the historical life of Jesus as one which transcended patriarchy in word and action, Asian women find that a "cosmic Christ" creates an opening for the salvific principles in other religious traditions which the "unique Christ*ization*" of the historical Jesus does not. Although Asian Christian women accept Jesus as the source of salvation and liberation for themselves, in their multi-religious context, a single savior figure seems implausible. [23] Hence Asian women do not have the same strong "uniqueness-of-Jesus" claims as their African and Latin American sisters.

While the foregoing reflects differences in the women's christological reflections, it also reveals a striking commonality apparent in the women's words and works: in none of them does the maleness of Jesus surface as a significant problem. [24] African women see the male Jesus not only as liberator but as true "Child of Women" in whom is equally revealed "the fullness of all that we know of perfect womanhood." [25] For Latin American women, the Risen Christ is first-born of all creatures, whose Spirit is poured out on both "sons and daughters" (Acts 2:18) and enables women and men equally to "speak, live and act *in persona Christi.*"[26] Asian women see the maleness of Jesus as a functional rather than an essential quality in Jesus; some even consider his maleness as a positive factor. "Jesus as a male put a period to the power of the patriarchal history."[27] In Asia the more significant problem is not that the one claimed to be a full and final disclosure of God is male but that he is human. From an Asian perspective, a total disclosure of God would have to include nature and the universe. A human being could not adequately reveal the fullness and totality of God.[28]

### *The Influence of Other Factors*
Although it is evident that context plays an important part in the development of the women's theological consciousness, it is equally evident in their documents and stories that it has not been the sole conditioning factor. Experience, exposure, and involvement are also influential. It was the "irruption" experience in Delhi which sparked the women's questioning of the male orientation in the emerging Third World theologies and which set them on the road toward doing collective theologizing from a women's perspective.

The individual women's stories paint a similar picture. Most of them acquired their interest in doing women's theology through some experience or involvement. It was her participation in the secular women's movement which was largely responsible for the development of Gnanadason's feminist[29] consciousness and commitment, and which later became the basis of her doing theology from a women's perspective in EATWOT. It was also experience—although in a *via negativa*—that led Oduyoye to become interested in, and begin to study, feminism. While in Selly Oaks, her research in Christian anthropology convinced her of its androcentric bias, and moved her to explore her own culture and language for elements that were either empowering or alienating for women. Through a different *via negativa*, Lee Park became convinced of the need to combine social analysis and a woman's perspective in her theological efforts. Firsthand experience of the sexist behavior of her male Korean compatriots led her to question the kind of democracy they were after, which put women in a subordinate role. She thus began to see that no movement for democracy or for reunification would be life-enhancing for the Korean people without the women's perspective.

Other types of experience, exposure, and involvement have been singled out by the women interviewed as factors that conditioned the development of their theological consciousness. Kwok, for instance, mentioned the helpful influence of a role model. Bingemer brought out the women's collective style of theologizing as having facilitated the women's corporate growth. Suffice it to say that while context plays a crucial role in the women's theological development, other factors[30] are also significant, which may account for commonalities among women from different contexts, and divergences among those from the same context.[31] In the following section, another factor will be examined in the light of the women's theological development: the EATWOT women's theological methodology and how it has functioned in their development.

### The Function of Methodology

The importance of methodology in theological formulation cannot be underestimated. From its inception, EATWOT chose a liberation methodology which placed commitment and involvement as the prior act of theology.[32] It was a reversal of the conventional way of theologizing which relied heavily on theories and principles, and it challenged the former conclusions about God and humanity. Thus our starting point, whether from below or from above, our reading of reality, and how we reflect upon it, determine to a large extent what we will say about God and God's designs for our world. Since our methodology conditions our conclusions in theology, it can be neither neutral nor arbitrary. EATWOT women have expanded the familiar framework of liberation theologies to include women's reality, an analysis of it, a faith reflection upon it, and a commitment to transform it. Having a common methodology has been a facilitating factor in the women's effort to develop a Third World theology from a women's perspective, but there are also some shortcomings that need the women's attention in a corporate way. A few of them will be examined below.

#### Analysis
At the Geneva dialogue with First World theologians, all agreed that there was need for a more comprehensive analysis of reality. Third World theologians, most women included, had hitherto focused on the political and economic oppression within their context. While

cultural and religious discrimination as well as gender domination
have since become part and parcel of Third World women's analysis,
racial oppression has not to the same extent, except in Africa. On the
three continents, racism has been rued and denounced in all major
EATWOT documents,[33] but how class, gender, and race intersect in
Third World women's lives has still not been adequately explored by
EATWOT women.[34] In the Buenos Aires women's conference, for
example, the Latin American women insisted that racism must be
addressed, but their essays gave little attention to the effects of racial
oppression on the lives of Latin American women. Yet Brazil, the
biggest and most populous of the Latin American countries has a
sizable black and indigenous population. In the 1989 Atlanta dialogue
between Third World women from both Third and First World
contexts, the question that arose in relation to racism and Third-
worldness was not resolved. The Afro-Americans felt a one-to-one
identification with the African women, but the African women argued
that race alone did not make a person "Third World"; analysis had to
go beyond skin color. The issue of race as it affects Third World
women evidently needs to be clarified and tackled more in depth.

Also lacking in the EATWOT women's corporate analysis is
sufficient attention to ecological issues and their effect on Third
World women. Because the Oaxtepec meeting focussed more on the
rc-interpretation of classical theological themes from the perspective
of Third World women, there was little reference to ecological
concerns either in the deliberations or in the final document. But
while concern for ecology as it relates to women's theology is indeed
present in some of the statements[35] and stories, it deserves greater
prominence in the EATWOT women's corporate work as a total
group. In their Buenos Aires statement, the Latin American women
saw the social sciences including ecology as woven "together with the
Bible, Tradition, and Life in a single tapestry."[36] In their Madras
document, the Asian women noted that "the greatest damage this
(colonial and neocolonial) model of development has done is to break
the bond between creation and humanity and this has legitimized
humankind's indiscriminate and aggressive abuse of the gifts of the
earth."[37]

These statements indicate that the ecological crisis and its effect
on women need more serious attention in the women's analysis and
theological reflection, for it is actually Third World women in general
who suffer most as a result of the ecological devastation and envi-

ronmental pollution taking place in the world.[38] While human beings are important, Third World women's theology cannot be only "people-oriented" as we claimed in Oaxtepec; it needs to encompass the whole of creation of which humanity is a part. Third World women's theology needs a creation-centered theology that is liberation-oriented as well. For while Third World women—their body, their health and well-being—have been the prime casualties of ecological and environmental abuse, they have been, at the same time, the worst victims of the economic crunch, becoming the world's poorest of the poor. In light of this dual plight of women in the Third World, women doing Third World theology become the most appropriate agents to promote a theology and spirituality[39] that is both creation-centered and liberation-oriented. Any dichotomization of the two is untenable in this "ecological, nuclear age."[40]

Without doubt, the women's analysis can be made more comprehensive. It could be further broadened and deepened, for example, with the use of existing feminist theories. It is curious to note that while EATWOT women demand "scientific seriousness" in their analysis of women's oppression, they have not made much use of the feminist theories in their gender analysis. It was only within the past few years that this lack was recognized by some of the EATWOT women. Some of the Latin American women interviewed by Tamez, and Tamez herself, acknowledged that the study of feminist theories as tools of analysis was imperative "for developing a more coherent and effective theology from women's perspective,"[41] but some of these theories may have to be reworked or reinterpreted. Feminist theories, those developed in the Third World in particular,[42] need to be considered seriously as part of women's theological effort. They should be examined, compared, assessed, and perhaps put together in a new way, for a more realistic and holistic analysis of Third World women's life and reality.

### Language

Language is part of methodology. It is a key factor in any theological enterprise since, as a science and an art, theology is never for private consumption but meant to be communicated. But for Third World women who do theology collectively, language has been a problem. How do we communicate our deepest thoughts about God, about life and death and our struggles, without a common language, without being able to use our mother tongue, without having to resort to a colonizer's idiom and to depend on interpreters? [43] While EATWOT women are determined not "to let semantic debate divert us from the course of our liberation,"[44] the language question remains unresolved.

Language has been a problem not only when Third World women get together on the tricontinental level.[45] It has been especially so for African women. Though African nations have local languages of their own,[46] a number of them use English or French as their official language.[47] Thus a language barrier exists when anglophones and francophones (not to mention the growing group of Portuguese speakers) have to meet or when they want to share their literature. Some African women have attempted to learn either French or English to facilitate communication, but more recently, other African women have begun to react to this insistence on speaking in a colonizer's idiom. If they have to learn a language, why not an African one? In the organizational meeting for the first biennial Institute of African Women in Religion and Culture, Swahili was used along with English and French, but not everyone could speak Swahili.

The use of French or English to articulate Third World women's theology is actually a more basic issue than the difficulty of communication or the additional expense of translators and interpreters: can we really use a First World language to formulate an authentic Third World theology? For language is not only a series of sounds and symbols, but carries with it a world view, a mental construct, a way of being and doing.[48] For Asian women, the dilemma is either to use one of the colonizers' languages (English), or not to theologize collectively at all.[49]

If EATWOT women persist in using a Western language or see no other alternative, then they must understand and empathize with Western feminist theologians' insistence on the use of non-sexist or inclusive language, especially in theology and liturgy. As Marjorie Proctor-Smith explains: "The critique itself is simple: exclusively or dominantly male language about God grants authority to men in a patriarchal culture and religion."[50] Many Third World women have not faced this as a problem because their mother tongues are not generally gender-differentiating, without gender-specific pronouns for God. Actually the problem is just more subtle but not absent. For most Third World Christians, the God of Jesus Christ is imaged as male.[51] The use of a neuter pronoun beclouds this fact, and subtly perpetuates male dominance.[52] The critique against the use of exclusive or dominantly male language outside of God-talk is simply a corollary of Proctor-Smith's statement above.

### Liberation Theology Framework

The early liberation theologies promoted by EATWOT all began as male-articulated theologies. This is true whether it was liberation theology in Latin America or in Africa, or minjung theology in Korea or black theology in South Africa. Males asked the questions, supplied the answers, developed the method, and determined the framework. Some of these liberation theologians talked or wrote about women, but it was always from an exclusively male perspective.[53] EATWOT women have begun to alert themselves about the danger of cooptation in doing theology from this (male) liberation framework, even while being conscious of incorporating women's perspective.[54] Knowing that the framework defines both the context and the content, a Korean woman theologian expressed one of her reservations about doing women's theology within the framework of liberation theology: "I don't know how much of the concept of the God of the liberation framework speaks to women's experience."[55] At the women's consultation in Buenos Aires, one of the participants issued this caution to the Latin American women:

> We are invited to increase the number of articles and books on . . . liberation theology. This effort does not liberate us; in fact, by encouraging us to do (male) scientific work, we fall into the same trap. We see ourselves succeeding as solitary women who have achieved recognition in a man's world. By doing this we simply perpetuate the present situation.[56]

An analogy can be made with regard to the temptation to do Third World women's theology within the framework set by Western feminist theology. Despite the fact that many women in the Third World had a negative first impression of the Western feminist movement, EATWOT women in general have acknowledged being inspired and influenced by Western feminist theologians and their works. This was especially evident in the interviews with the Asian women, but other EATWOT women have been similarly appreciative. As Tamez has attested: "Feminist theologians have done theology and hermeneutics in a deeper way, and we are reaping the richness of their theological production."[57] While EATWOT women have found elements in feminist theology both instructive and liberating, some of them have begun to sense the danger of becoming dependent on the Western feminist model for developing Third World women's theology. Thus Gnanadason warns: "We could be swept off our feet by Western feminist theologians. We have to be grounded in our own context and in the lives of our own women."[58]

This warning should be taken seriously, for indeed feminist theology was developed in the West, and Western women have defined the parameters of the discipline based on their own history, context, culture, and experience. In the Geneva dialogue with First World theologians, the Third World women saw that liberation made different demands on them than on First World women. For Third World women, there was no way of addressing the issue of sexism without taking into account the people's poverty and neocolonial condition, as well as the people's struggle for liberation in their own countries.[59] As the Korean women later wrote in their report for the women's Madras meeting in 1990: "Women's liberation must be worked out simultaneouly with the national issues which also affect men and children. . . Liberated women in an unfree society cannot enjoy full humanity."[60] Chung has this additional comment to make: "Liberation is different because our pain and struggles are different, and even our bodies are different. First World bodies do not usually starve; neither are they usually tortured by the military. nor mutilated in unsafe factories, nor endangered by political unheavals."[61]

It is clear that EATWOT women have gained much from both the male-developed Third World liberation theology and First World feminist theology,[62] and wish to remain in dialogical relationship with both. Nevertheless, EATWOT women need not be limited by the framework set by these theologies, but should gradually produce their own. Afro-American women in the United States understood this limitation when they decided to call theirs a "womanist" theology instead of simply "black" or simply "feminist."[63] In a similar vein, Hispanic women in the United States chose to call themselves *n ujeristas* to mark their distinctiveness.[64] It was propitious—though the implications were not entirely apparent at the time—that the initial members of the Women's Commission decided to call theirs "a theology from a Third World women's perspective." It may not be the best title, but at least it is clear that it is Third World women who would define its framework and whose accountability would be primarily to Third World women. Meanwhile, it is still the EATWOT women's hope that one day more relevant and inclusive theologies for Third World Christians will come to pass.

### The Role of EATWOT

Without doubt EATWOT has played a decisive role in the growth of Third World women's theological consciousness. The communal way of theologizing and the cross-fertilization afforded by the association's intercontinental conferences have enabled EATWOT women to enlarge their theological horizon, to sharpen their analysis of the unjust global order, and to strengthen their commitment to the promotion of God's liberating Reign. It was through their involvement in EATWOT's Women's Commission that a number of the women began consciously doing theology from a Third World women's perspective. Bingemer and Mananzan, for example, acknowledged this in their stories.[65]

It is true that EATWOT has helped the women, but so have the EATWOT women helped the Association. While not all the positive changes in the Association can be attributed to the presence of women, it can be said that since the establishment of the Women's Commission, there has been a notable change in the attitudes and practices within EATWOT. There is less evidence of the condescending and trivializing behavior of the past. Instead there is a gradual openness among the men (even mingled with some timidity) to dialogue with the women on women's issues. This was obvious in the interviews Tamez had with the Latin American male liberation theologians, who recognized that the oppression of women is not just a women's concern: the macho mentality which grants privileges to males is damaging to men as well.[66]

Dialogue between EATWOT women and men has also begun in Asia. In ATC III in 1989, they discussed the issue of sexuality together for the first time in an EATWOT event.[67] The following year, in preparation for the women's meeting in Madras, Indian women and men held an all-day dialogue on such issues as patriarchy, women's reality, and the theology of sacrifice imposed on Indian women. The men admitted the shortcomings of their analysis which did not recognize patriarchy as "the system that keeps all forms of oppression intact" and which failed to consider the feminist vision "as an alternative political vision."[68]

With this gradual openness of the part of EATWOT men, the women hope to see a subsequent incorporation of the women's perspective in EATWOT's theologies and an eventual change in its way of doing theology. That women have a different viewpoint to offer was evident, for example, when the Indian male and female EATWOT members shared their views on women's reality. While the men tended to idealize "the long-suffering patience and compassion-ate beauty of their mothers—women who have most often left a deep spiritual impression on their lives,[69] the women theologians saw the long-suffering patience of women not something to be idealized but something "to be challenged that needs the transforming power of the Gospel."[70]

The EATWOT women are still in the process of developing their methodology; however, they recognize certain emerging features that could enhance EATWOT's way of doing theology. As they wrote in their final document in Oaxtepec: "The passionate and compassion-ate way in which women do theology is a rich contribution to theological science."[71] The theological point of departure is not only the "praxis of justice" but also the "praxis of caring." The relational is as important as the rational, for the oppression against which we all struggle is ultimately a matter of unjust, unequal, and uncaring relationships. Thus Third World women stress community and solidarity. Doing theology with passion and compassion means doing it not only with the mind, but also with the heart, the body. Thus for the Asian women, a conducive atmosphere and group processes that involve the senses and bodily movements are important in collective theologizing;[72] for the Latin Americans, a sense of humor, joy, and celebration. For the Africans, women's contribution must be "vital and lively." While these features are not totally absent from men's theologizing, EATWOT women feel they are not emphasized enough.

A striking example of what EATWOT women are trying to do theologically and methodologically was given by Chung in her pres-entation of the theological theme, "Come Holy Spirit, Renew the Whole Creation," before the WCC Assembly in Canberra on February 8, 1991. Expressing herself not only through words but through a creative blend of dance and sound, collective movement and visual art, together with a troupe of Korean and aboriginal performers, Chung enabled the assembly to "feel, touch, and taste the concrete bodily historical presence of the Holy Spirit" in their midst.[73]

Writing his impressions of the Assembly, K.C. Abraham, then vice president of EATWOT, had high praises for Chung's presentation, calling it "a challenge to our mode of theologizing."[74]

While it is true that a gradual change in attitude has occurred in EATWOT due to women's initiative, there is still room for much improvement in the realm of practice.[75]  As a recent example, the four major speakers finally  chosen for the EATWOT general assembly in 1992 were all men while women were left to be respondents.  Such a  decision is not defensible at this time of EATWOT's history; it negates in part its advances and puts into question its credibility as an association dedicated to "total human liberation."

EATWOT women remain hopeful, nevertheless, and look forward to the day when EATWOT women and men can work together in partnership toward more relevant and inclusive theologies for the Third World.  But "a more inclusive Third World Theology" is beginning to take on a different meaning for EATWOT women.  As they grow in ecological consciousness, they no longer simply think in terms of incorporating both men's and women's perspectives, or including in a respectful way the concerns and challenges of struggling groups we have hitherto placed in the margin of our EATWOT theologies.[76]  It means encompassing the whole of creation, which also eagerly awaits its liberation (see Romans 8:19-23).[77]  "Third World" also acquires a new significance.  While it remains that part of the world characterized by poverty and oppression, it is also that part of the globe which has suffered most from ecological devastation, from the "wanton human domination of the natural world."[78]

The day of relevant and inclusive Third World theologies may not be too far in the distance.  This will not mean a departure from, but rather an extension of, EATWOT's theological direction.  While the Oaxtepec assembly document still speaks of "liberation struggles" and "full humanity for all," it also speaks of "a spiritual theology which will encompass the cosmos" and "a new earth, socially and ecologically sound and whole."[79]  Liberation thus takes on a new meaning and a new but related praxis,[80] which will have implications not only for our theology but for our christology and soteriology as well.[81]  Life and community, both central to EATWOT theology, will have to be seen anew; so will the Bible.

EATWOT's future will be decided by the next general assembly in 1992.  In Nairobi, the assembly will evaluate the association's past five years and determine its work and direction for the next half-decade.  This includes the Women's Commission as well.  It is hoped that this present study which examined the contribution of EATWOT women to the association and to Third World theology will help to guide that future.  The conclusions, hopes, and recommendations based on the study will form the content of the final chapter.

# CHAPTER SEVEN

## CHARTING THE FUTURE

This study was designed to trace the origins and development of Third World women's theological consciousness within EATWOT. It has shown that while EATWOT women are not the only ones doing theology from a Third World women's perspective, they have made a notable contribution to this venture. Third World women are no longer voiceless or invisible in the theological world. Their word is beginning to be recognized, heard, and read not only in the Third World but in the First World as well.[1] From being mere theological object, they have become producer and subject of theology. This final chapter contains the significant conclusions from the study.

### Twelve Findings of the Study

While a number of conclusions can be drawn from the present work, only the major ones are listed here:

First: Third World women's theology is necessarily pluralistic and multi-faceted. Given the wide variety of context and experience, it is evident that Third World women do not and cannot speak with one voice.

Second: Speaking from their distinct experience and perspective, Third World women have a different word to say than their Third World brothers or First World sisters. Thus they have their own unique contribution to make to theology which would be the poorer and incomplete without it.

Third: Third World women theologians have been greatly helped by the organizational support of EATWOT, especially through its

Women's Commission. Their experience shows that such support is necessary in order for women theologians to enrich, encourage, and challenge one another, as well as to work collectively in common theological projects. However, their experience also shows that without proper coordination and effective channels of mutual support and communication within and among the continents, collective work can be unduly hindered.

Fourth: Though EATWOT women have traveled far since the establishment of the Women's Commission, they still have miles to go in their collective theological journey. They need further occasions for exchange and cross-fertilization, for clarification and deepening, for mutual critique and support in order to continue their journey.

Fifth: The EATWOT experience suggests that an opportunity for exchange and networking among Third World women not only enlarges their theological vision but also leads to greater flowering of their talents and potential. The unique gifts women bring to theology must be recognized and nurtured not only by EATWOT but by their particular communities, congregations, and institutions.

Sixth: The relational factor is most essential in the EATWOT women's emerging methodology. Thus they see no less than a relationship of mutual respect and dialogical partnership with their Third World brothers as they work together toward relevant and inclusive Third World theologies. They envision the same relationship with their Third World sisters in the First World in their common tasks and with their First World sisters in works of solidarity.

Seventh: Doing theology as Third World women is a specific way of struggling for life and justice that is intimately linked to ministry. It is, in fact, in itself a ministry, and not a separate or marginal activity. Thus whether their involvement is in Church communities or in women's movements, in the classroom or in the field, Third World women doing theology are in ministry, at the service of all who struggle for wholeness of life and liberation. In this way of being in ministry, Third World women can serve as role models for the coming generation of women theologians in the Third World.

Eighth: Both the work of reconstruction and construction are essential in the work of doing theology from a Third World women's perspective. Not either/or but both: both the reformulation of classical themes and the formulation of new ones that stem from context and culture are equally indispensable. Indeed there are sources waiting to be tapped,[2] stories to be told, traditions and histories to be reclaimed.

Ninth: As liberation takes on a new meaning for Third World women, their emerging theologies and spiritualities will have to go beyond the goal of "total human liberation" to include the integrity of the whole of creation. The "cry for life"[3] is not only the Third World's but all creation's as well.

Tenth: Because doing theology demands a commitment to transform reality, EATWOT women must also work together towards an alternative political vision which they can translate into action to bring about a renewed Church, a new society, and a new earth.[4]

Eleventh: If EATWOT women truly believe that it is "women from the base who are best equipped to speak on Third World women's reality," then it is important to have more direct participation in grassroots and secular women's movements which struggle for life and justice.[5] The main accountability of Third World women's theology is to these women who represent the majority of women in the Third World. Further, EATWOT women should also try to develop, in collaboration with other women, indigenous feminist theories which would help to give direction to women's movements for liberation.

Twelfth and lastly: Third World women are the principal resources as well as the ultimate critics of the theologies EATWOT women are developing. EATWOT women need to explore ways of communicating to them other than through the written word which has its obvious limitations in the Third World. There must be more viable ways of enabling greater numbers of Third World women to judge whether the emerging theologies articulated by EATWOT women are authentically theirs as well.

### Recommended Tasks for the Future

In light of the foregoing conclusions, some important tasks remain. Henceforth, is is recommended that

(1) as they engage in doing theology, EATWOT women refine their methodology,[6] with more serious attention given to analysis of language and racism, and clarify for themselves what it means to theologize from "a Third World women's perspective";

(2) in their work toward an inclusive theology that is both creation-centered and liberation-oriented, EATWOT be in dialogue not only with other faiths and ideologies but with indigenous religions

and cultures as well;

(3) in order to reach a wider range of Third World women, the women in EATWOT begin to formulate their theology in creative, innovative ways that touch both hearts and minds: through art and poetry, through folk songs and drama, through the use of radio plays, video films, and movies. As radio and television have a more popular appeal, they will be more effective than the printed word in the Third World.

Because of the limited nature of the present study, it is evident that further research is necessary for a more profound understanding of Third World women's theological contribution. The present study focussed on the history of Third World women's theological journey, on commonalities and differences, and on the factors that helped or hindered the women's progress. It is therefore recommended that a succeeding study be made on the *content* of Third World women's emerging theologies, that is, the results of their reconstruction of classical themes as well as the product of their theological investigation of issues that affect women's lives in the Third World today.

It is likewise urged that a companion research be done on the convergences and divergences of Third World women's theologies as they are developed in both the Third and First World contexts. This would be helpful in fostering deeper bonding and solidarity among Third World women everywhere, as well as a better appreciation of their particular contribution in the creation of a new society and a new earth.

## Implications for the Future

The collective theological journey of EATWOT women has just begun, but they are determined to go on. They know that the road will be long and tortuous. Like most long journeys in the Third World, there are no guarantees of smooth roads or clear directions or freedom from risks and obstacles along the way. Having begun their journey without established road signs, EATWOT women are determined to continue creating their own as they move on.

EATWOT women are also aware that they will meet with pain and opposition in their journey. In a world still governed by patriarchal norms and values, women doing theology are not only suspect, they are also a threat. EATWOT women realize there will be resistance along the way—from Church and society, from men and women alike.

But EATWOT women are not dismayed. Like those who have to travel far and long in the Third World, they do not ask whether the road will be smooth and easy. Rather they ask: Is a long and difficult journey worth the risk and the pain? If it is empowering for women, if it brings wholeness to humanity, if it fosters respect for creation, if it transforms Church and society, then for the Third World women in EATWOT, the long and difficult journey ahead is worth it.

# AFTERWORD

## THE JOURNEY CONTINUES

Twenty-nine EATWOT women from Africa, Asia, Latin America and from among the U.S. Minorities met together in Nairobi, Kenya, from January 5 to 13, 1992. The occasion was the Association's third General Assembly.[1] It is evident from the preceding chapters that general assemblies have been important landmarks in the life of EATWOT women. The Nairobi assembly was no exception. Thus a word about it becomes a necessary postscript to this book on EATWOT women.

For the general membership, the assembly was a historic occasion that brought EATWOT back to its African beginnings: it was in Africa that EATWOT was born.[2] For the EATWOT women, however, it was historic in yet another sense: for us who were there it was a break-through in EATWOT assemblies.

We recalled the disillusionment and confrontations that took place at the founding assembly in Dar es Salaam,[3] the tensions that led to the "irruption within the irruption" in Delhi,[4] and the conflictive atmosphere that prevailed in Oaxtepec.[5] By way of contrast, the spirit in Nairobi was one of openness, cooperation, and mutual respect; one which granted the women full and effective voice for the first time in an EATWOT assembly.[6] It was an empowering experience for the women.

As EATWOT members, we felt we were listened to individually and collectively, and we were being taken seriously.[7] The difference in the attitude of our male colleagues was notable: they were more conscious about using inclusive language and apologizing when they did not, and they did not hesitate to show their appreciation and solidarity. It was very moving when, at the final liturgy, they knelt before the group and asked forgiveness of the women for their past insensitive attitudes and behavior.

The women, for their part, created an impact on the assembly by the caliber and extent of their participation. What was initially considered an error, inviting only male speakers for the three assembly topics and relegating women to the role of respondents, turned out to be a *"felix culpa."* One by one the women respondents ably critiqued from a Third World women's perspective, both positively and negatively, the presentations on Spirituality, Christology, and Commitment.[8] These three topics were the major sub-themes of the assembly theme: "A Cry for Life: The Spirituality of the Third World." The women spoke with seriousness and clarity, offering fresh insights drawn from their experience as Third World women, and all the while standing on solid theological ground.

Three women deserve special mention. Ivone Gebara was asked to be one of two panelist to replace Gustavo Gutierrez as keynote speakers when he could not attend the assembly. Gebara's social analysis, which was based on the type of garbage people disposed of, demonstrated EATWOT women's capacity for original thinking. Teresa Okure showed the women's capability for bold explorations when she announced her projected work on "Jesus as Mother." Bernard Mcube, a religious sister and newcomer to EATWOT, electrified the assembly and was the most applauded delegate because of her "speeches" from the heart about the South African reality, and her impassioned and fearless denunciation of injustices within the Church and her country. In addition, the Asian women who constituted a strong voice at the assembly, with ease and grace displayed their ability to theologize without words in a women's liturgy.

The women were delighted to note the move toward cosmic spirituality at the assembly,[9] and they welcomed the creative display of new modes of expressing theology, which as EATWOT women they were advocating and promoting. The daily "recaps,"[10] done entertainingly by Karl Gaspar and his partners through song, poetry, drama, a TV newscast, and a sing-along, were veritable theological reflections in themselves. The worship services were replete with symbolism and rituals from different parts of the Third World. An Afro-Brazilian ritual opened us up to receiving vital energy from the earth and sharing it with one another. Instead of the usual Bible study, the Asian delegation presented a scriptural study of the major religious traditions of Asia. Their presentation brought out the ultimate message of concern for neighbor found in these scriptures by using a combination of tableau, mime, and an historical/analytical commentary.[11]

The EATWOT women had an evening together to prepare for the business session of the assembly. Sharing regional updates and hopes for the future, the women realized that despite having gone separate ways during the past five years, their bonding as EATWOT women remained firm. At the same time they recognized that now as in the past, they needed more than bonding to achieve the goal they had set for themselves as a Commission ten years ago: there was still much concerted work to do. Thus they resolved they would recommend to the assembly the continuance of the Women's Commission.

They also agreed to appeal to the incoming Executive Committee to restore the position of international coordinator as well as to invite more women speakers for future EATWOT conferences; furthermore, they would ask the editor of *Voices from the Third World* to devote an entire issue on women. For the Women's Commission itself, the women concurred on the following recommendations;[12]

—to work toward a common program;

—to have greater intercontinental exchange;

—to have further dialogue between the women from
the Third World continents and from the U.S. minorities;

—to have further dialogue among minority women throughout the world;

—to reformulate the theme proposed by the Planning Committee for the dialogue between EATWOT women and First World women theologians. The EATWOT women felt the theme "Re-Imaging Hospitality: Prophetic Voices from the South and North" did not speak adequately to the situation of the majority of Third World women. [13]

At the business meeting on the last day, the assembly delegates unanimously voted for the continuance of the Women's Commission and gave it the prerogative to choose its own program and organizational structure.[14] Moreover, the delegates elected four women out of a total of seven members to the new Executive Committee, making women the majority of EATWOT officers for the first time.[15]

The assembly was not all rosy, however. The women regretted the limited time to plan together for the next five years. A few wondered if the absence of conflict was actually positive or negative. As one member remarked afterwards, "What if we had devoted the entire assembly to a feminist critique of spirituality and religion?" [16] Some women were disappointed that the issues raised at the plenaries were not critiqued from the gender perspective. For example, the discussion on socialism, its demise in Eastern Europe and its effect on EATWOT would have benefitted from such a critique. Both men and women missed having an exposure to, and a deeper analysis of, the Kenyan context.

Nairobi was not a perfect assembly, but the experience of the EATWOT women there gave them the confidence and determination to carry on their theological journey together. They left the assembly feeling empowered and renewed. Their bonding as EATWOT sisters was strengthened; at the same time they knew they had to go beyond bonding if their theological journey in the next five years is to take them closer to their dream.

# NOTES

◆◆◆

## INTRODUCTION

1 It will also be referred to as "the Association."

2 The doctoral dissertation/project resulting from the study is entitled "The Development of Women's Theological Consciousness within the Ecumenical Association of Third World Theologians." It was presented to the Committee for Advanced Pastoral Studies, San Francisco Theological Seminary, San Anselmo, California, in January of 1992, in partial fulfillment of the requirements for the degree Doctor of Ministry.

3 There is of course no such thing as an "objective" history. It is always written from the historian's own perspective.

4 I remain open, however, to a dialogue with those who have a different interpretation of EATWOT's history.

5 Theological Education Fund, *Ministry in Context* (London: TEF, 1972), 20.

6 Ibid.

7 It is admitted that all theologies in the past, consciously or unconsciously, were contextual, that is, born out of social conditions and needs of a particular time and place. In the past, however, theologians did not take context seriously and created theologies by using doctrines and abstractions, rather than their concrete context, as their starting point. The resulting theology was then taught as "universal theology" applicable to all other times and contexts. The best example is European theology elaborated out of the Western European tradition and proposed as universal theology. For other versions of contextual theology, see Stephen Bevans, "Models of Contextual Theology," *Missiology: An International Review* 13 (April 1985). Along with earlier writings, this article has been revised and expanded into a volume with the same title published by Orbis Books, Maryknoll, NY, 1992.

8 Like the French commoners who "faced off against the clergy and aristocracy, these nations wanted freedom, dignity and control over their own destinies." William J. Grimm, "The `Third' World," *America* 162 (May 5, 1990):

449.

9 At that time the term 'Third World' was taken to mean the countries outside the industrialized capitalist countries of Europe, North America, Japan, Australia, and New Zealand (which became known as the 'First World'), and the socialist countries of Europe, including the USSR (which became known as the 'Second World'). See "Final Statement," in *The Emergent Gospel: Theology from the Underside of History*, ed. Sergio Torres and Virginia Fabella (Maryknoll, N.Y.: Orbis Books, 1978), 260.

10 In the words of Sergio Torres, EATWOT's first executive secretary, "The concept of Third World is, in the first place, not limited to geographical space . . . There are people who live in Hong Kong or Bolivia who do not identify ideologically with the Third World . . . their hearts, their interests, their futures are linked with the dominant classes of the world." Torres, "Introduction," in Torres and Fabella, *Emergent Gospel,* ix.

11 For a description and brief analysis of this condition, see "Final Statement of the Fifth EATWOT Conference, New Delhi, August 17-19, 1981," in *Irruption of the Third World: Challenge to Theology*, ed. Virginia Fabella and Sergio Torres (Maryknoll, N.Y.: Orbis Books, 1983), 192-195.

12 See footnote no. 8 above. In his article, Grimm goes on to explain why today the phrase only serves to obscure reality and should be discontinued. A position similar to Grimm's is taken by Robert J. Samuelson, "End of the Third World," *Newsweek* (July 30, 1990): 4. The events in the countries in eastern Europe have introduced new reasons for questioning the relevancy of the term "Third World."

13 See, for example, "Introduction," in *With Passion and Compassion: Third World Women Doing Theology*, ed. Virginia Fabella and Mercy Amba Oduyoye (Maryknoll, N.Y.: Orbis Books, 1988), ix. See also chap. 1, footnote no. 42 below.

14 J. Russell Chandran, "A Methodological Approach to Third World Theology," in Fabella and Torres, *Irruption*, 80.

15 The original work towards a Third World women's theology written from an Asian perspective was by Marianne Katoppo, Indonesian theologian. See Marianne Katoppo, *Compassionate and Free: An Asian Woman's Theology* (Maryknoll, N.Y.: Orbis Books, 1980), first published by the World Council of Churches, Geneva, in 1979. See also Mercy Amba Oduyoye, *Hearing and Knowing: Theological Reflections on Christianity in Africa* (Maryknoll, N.Y.: Orbis Books, 1986), especially chap. 10, and Ivone Gebara and Maria Clara Bingemer, *Mary, Mother of God, Mother of the Poor* (Maryknoll, N.Y.: Orbis Books, 1989). Besides *Passion and Compassion*, collections of essays published in English within the past seven years with significant contributions from EATWOT women are: John S. Pobee and Barbel Von Wartenberg-Potter, eds. *New Eyes for Reading* (Geneva: World Council of Churches, 1986); Letty M. Russell, Kwok Pui-lan, Ada Maria Isasi-Diaz, Katie Geneva Cannon, eds. *Inheriting Our Mothers' Gardens: Feminist Theology in Third World Perspective* (Philadelphia: Westminister Press, 1988);

Elsa Tamez, ed. *Through Her Eyes: Women's Theology from Latin America* (Maryknoll, N.Y.: Orbis Books, 1989); Virginia Fabella and Sun Ai Lee Park, eds. *We Dare to Dream: Doing Theology as Asian Women* (Maryknoll, N.Y.: Orbis Books, 1990); Mercy Amba Oduyoye and Musumbi R. A. Kanyoro, eds. *The Will to Arise: Women, Tradition, and the Church in Africa* (Maryknoll, N.Y.: Orbis Books, 1992).

Two doctoral dissertations on Asian women and theology by EATWOT members which have been published are Chung Hyun Kyung, *Struggle to Be the Sun Again: Introducing Asian Women's Theology* (Maryknoll, N.Y.: Orbis Books, 1990), and Kwok Pui-lan, *Chinese Women and Christianity 1860-1927* (Atlanta: Scholars Press, 1992). A third dissertation related to Asian women's theology is Elizabeth Tapia's, "The Contribution of Philippine Christian Women to Asian Women's Theology" (Claremont Graduate School, 1989).

## CHAPTER ONE: A MOVEMENT NAMED EATWOT

[1] "Final Statement of the Fifth EATWOT Conference, New Delhi, August 17-49, 1981," in Fabella and Torres, *Irruption*, 200.

[2] During the 1980s, the more economically advanced Third World countries in Asia won the new designation of "newly industrializing countries" (NICs). These are Hong Kong, South Korea, Singapore, and Taiwan.

[3] For common features of "underdeveloped" countries and different explanations regarding "underdevelopment," see Leonardo Boff, "What are Third World Theologies?" in *Theologies of the Third World: Convergences and Differences*, Concilium, ed. Leonardo Boff and Virgil Elizondo (Edingurgh: T. & T. Clark Ltd., 1988), 3-14. See also "Final Statement," in Torres and Fabella, *Emergent Gospel*, 259-264.

[4] As quoted in Adeolu Adegbola, "Christian Responsibility in the Political Economy of Africa," *The Ecumenical Review* 37 (January 1985): 89.

[5] Ibid.

[6] See "Final Statement," in Torres and Fabella, *Emergent Gospel*, 263.

[7] Important UNCTAD sessions were held in New Delhi (1968), Santiago (1972), and Nairobi (1976).

[8] The failure of UNCTAD to bring forth a new economic order was due to the resistance and opposition not only of industrialized countries but also of the powerful and affluent elite in some poor countries of the world.

[9] The significance of these two events is noted in the final statement of the Ecumenical Dialogue of Third World Theologians in August 1976, at the conclusion of which EATWOT was formed. See Torres and Fabella, *Emergent Gospel*, 264.

[10] See *Everyone's United Nations*, 9th ed., (New York: United Nations Publication, 1979), 122-125. See also Sergio Torres, "Opening Address," in Kofi Appiah-Kubi and Sergio Torres, eds. *African Theology En Route* (Maryknoll, N.Y.: Orbis Books, 1979), 7-9.

11 Convened by Pope John XXIII on Oct. 11, 1962, it ended on Dec. 8, 1965. It is notable that in his 1963 encyclical *Pacem in Terris* Pope John stated: "Since women are becoming more conscious of their human dignity, they will not tolerate being treated as mere material instruments, but demand rights befitting a human person both in domestic and in public life." See David J. O'Brien and Thomas A. Shannon, eds. *Renewing the Earth* (Garden City, N.Y.: Image Books, 1977), 134.

12 O'Brien and Shannon, *Renewing the Earth*, 307.

13 For overviews of these two assemblies from different perspectives, see the 40th anniversary issue of *The Ecumenical Review* 40 (July-October 1988), 344-347, 354-356, 377-378, 394-396. The issue is entitled: *Commemorating Amsterdam 1948: 40 Years of the World Council of Churches*. For an assessment of the women's conference, see Marga Buhrig, "Uppsala 1968—Berlin 1974—JPIC Convocation 1990?" in the same issue, 396-398. JPIC stands for Justice, Peace, and the Integrity of Creation.

14 For an outline of the documents on justice and peace, see Peter J. Henriot, Edward De Berri and Michael J. Schultheis, *Catholic Social Teaching, Our Best-Kept Secret* (Maryknoll, N.Y.: Orbis Books, 1988), 104-108. For an insightful overview of the Medellin event, see Penny Lernoux, "The Long Path to Puebla," in *Puebla and Beyond*, ed. John Eagleson and Philip Scharper (Maryknoll, N.Y.: Orbis Books, 1979), 3-27.

15 P.A. Kalilombe, "Self-Reliance of the African Church: A Catholic Perspective" in Appiah-Kubi and Torres, *African Theology*, 36; see also footnote no. 1 on p. 58 of the same book.

16 Gustavo Gutierrez, *A Theology of Liberation* (Maryknoll, N.Y.: Orbis Books, 1973). Originally published as *Teologia de la liberacion, Perspectivas*, by CEP, Lima in 1971.

17 James Cone, *Black Theology and Black Power* (New York: Seabury Press, 1970).

18 Enrique Dussel, "Theologies of the `Periphery' and the `Centre': Encounter or Confrontation?" in *Different Theologies, Common Responsibility: Babel or Pentecost?*, Concilium, ed. Claude Geffre, Gustavo Gutierrez and Virgil Elizondo (Edinburgh: T. & T. Clark Ltd., 1984), 88.

19 See editor's note in O. K. Bimwenyi, "The Origins of EATWOT," *Voices from the Third World* 4 (December 1981): 19. Among Bimwenyi's friends was Francois Houtart, professor at the University of Louvain, who played an important part during EATWOT's birthing years and early infancy.

20 The coordinators chosen were O. K. Bimwenyi for Africa, D. S. Amalorpavadass for Asia, and Enrique Dussel for Latin America.

21 The introductory circular was produced by Bimwenyi and Dussel, together with Stan Lourdusami from Asia. See Sergio Torres Gonzalez, "Dar-es-Salaam 1976," in Boff and Elizondo, *Convergences and Differences*, 109.

22 Bimwenyi, "Origins of EATWOT," *Voices* 4, 20. It contains a summary of correspondence which reveals a broad consensus regarding the topics. Bimwenyi classifies these under three general headings: (1) methodo-

logical problems in contextual theology, (2) Christianity and national religions, and (3) intra-ecclesial and .pastoral problems.

[23] One Church leader who held a different view was Yap Kim Hao, the then general secretary of the CCA. He believed in the "responsibility of existing ecumenical organizations . . . in the Third World to initiate and sponsor ecumenical dialogue for Third World theologians." Moreover, he felt that Asians were not ready for a tricontinental colloquium: "For dialogue to take place meaningfully and creatively among Third World theologians, the Asians and Africans especially will have to discover and articulate its (sic) own theology. This is what CCA is striving to do . . ." See Yap Kim Hao to Chandran, July 15, 1976. Dar es Salaam Conference (First Five-year Term), EATWOT Archives.

[24] For practical reasons, A. Ngindu Mushete replaced Bimwenyi as African coordinator while Sergio Torres replaced Enrique Dussel as Latin American coordinator. D. S. Amalorpavadass, the Asian coordinator, could not attend the Louvain meeting but met with Ngindu and Torres in Nairobi. Torres was the most suitable person to replace Dussel as coordinator for Latin America. He was stationed in New York as Executive Secretary of Theology in the Americas (TIA) so he had a convenient base and access to facilities. A year earlier, he had organized the Detroit dialogue between Latin American liberation theologians and "minority" theologians from the U.S.A. After that, he was asked by the Maryknoll Fathers to coordinate a similar conference between Latin American liberation theologians and African theologians, which was later superseded in favor of the broader dialogue.

[25] Two from each continent were represented on the committee, with Chandran as president and Torres as executive secretary.

[26] Henceforth to be referred to as the (Dar) Dialogue.

[27] There was one representative from the U.S. black minority group.

[28] Though assistance was given by European and North American churches, funding agencies, and religious institutions, as well as by two support committees, these groups kept a respectful distance when it came to planning the agenda for the Dialogue.

[29] See Dussel, "Periphery," in Geffre, Gutierrez and Elizondo, *Babel or Pentecost*, 92-93; also footnote no. 53 on p. 97 for what might be termed an exception.

[30] For full coverage of this event, see Sergio Torres and John Eagleson, eds. *Theology in the Americas* (Maryknoll, N.Y.: Orbis Books, 1976).

[31] Torres explains why Tanzania was chosen: "Its arid regions, its droughts, and its poverty are a challenge to the whole world. This country identifies with its leader, President Julius Nyerere, and with his program of *ujamaa* to combat underdevelopment . . . which combines elements from both the Christian and the best African traditions, (and) constitutes a real source of attraction and admiration for all those who ask questions about...the role of Christians in developing countries." Torres, "Introduction," in Torres and Fabella, *Emergent Gospel*, viii.

[32] As a member of the TIA staff at that time, I was assigned to help in

organizing the Dialogue.

[33] "Communique," in Torres and Fabella, *Emergent Gospel*, 272.

[34] From Africa, A. Ngindu Mushete, Charles Nyamiti, K. A. Dickson, Edward Fashole-Luke, Patrick A. Kalilombe, Kofi Appiah-Kubi; from Asia, D. S. Amalorpavadass (deceased), J. R. Chandran, Carlos Abesamis, Lynn de Silva (deceased), Mark Fang, Tissa Balasuriya, Peter K. H. Lee; from Latin America, Hugo Assmann, Beatriz Melano Couch, Enrique Dussel, Gustavo Gutierrez, Gerardo Viviers (replacing Jose Miguez-Bonino), Sergio Torres; from the Caribbean, Harold Sitahal (replacing Idris Hamid). Maurice Assad came from Egypt as a representative of the Orthodox Church in Africa; C. T. Vivian represented the U.S. Black minority. Among the invited but who could not attend was K. H. Ting from China.

[35] The original list of invitees contained only names of male theologians. The support committees pressured the dialogue organizers about women's participation. In the end, the fear of getting flak from the funding agencies led to the decision to invite a woman.

[36] Couch's paper was published under the title, "New Visions of the Church in Latin America: A Protestant View." See Torres and Fabella, *Emergent Gospel*, 193-227. In her entire essay, Couch refers to Latin American women in one sole paragraph, which largely gave credit to Emilio Castro for his "prophetic" role in being the "first to see the need to incorporate women into the struggle for liberation." Ibid., 207. Castro had called a meeting of Latin American women at the same time that men gathered for a Church and Society assembly in Piriapolis, Uruguay in 1967.

[37] Torres, "Dar-es-Salaam," in Boff and Elizondo, *Convergences and Differences*, 110.

[38] Their fear was not unfounded. "Some Latin American theologians seemed excessively sure of their own theology, showed no real inclination to listen to others, and did not conceal their intention and desire to put forward the Latin American theology of liberation as a universal model for the entire Third World." Ibid., 113.

[39] "Final Statement," in Torres and Fabella, *Emergent Gospel*, 271.

[40] For results of the Dialogue, see Torres and Fabella, *Emergent Gospel*. Not all the papers presented could be included because of space limitations.

[41] "Communique," in ibid., 273.

[42] The members debated the use of 'Third World' in the name of the new association. "The expression 'Third World' is not a happy one, but it was accepted as more adequately descriptive of the main concern of the association than any other term." J. R. Chandran, "Message to the Conference," in *The Challenge of Basic Christian Communities*, ed. Sergio Torres and John Eagleson (Maryknoll, N.Y.: Orbis Books, 1981), xvi. In a later interview by the NCC News, Chandran commented: "They call us the Third World, but we should be called 'the two-thirds world' because we contain the vast majority of the world's people." But some EATWOT members resist the term 'two thirds world' precisely because it suggests numbers rather than quality of life.

43 "Communique," in Torres and Fabella, *Emergent Gospel*, 273.

44 Ibid. Also stated are the conditions for membership: "Those born and normally serving in one of the Third World countries" or "members of the dispersion from Africa, Asia, and Latin America involved in some form of doing theology."

45 The foregoing description of the two features is taken from the author's article, "Emerging Third World Theologies," in *Kalinangan*, 3 (September 1983): 14. *Kalinangan* is the quarterly publication of the Institute of Religion and Culture (P.O. Box 131, Ermita, Manila, Philippines).

46 See "Final Statement" in Torres and Fabella, *Emergent Gospel*, 269-271.

47 Torres, "Dar-es-Salaam," in Boff and Elizondo, *Convergences and Differences*, 108.

48 James Cone, "Ecumenical Association of Third World Theologians," *Ecumenical Trends* 14 (September 1985): 119.

49 Torres, "Dar-es-Salaam," in Boff and Elizondo, *Convergences and Differences*, 108. Hosted by Indonesian President Sukarno, the Bandung Conference of African and Asian states in 1955 openly declared an anti-colonialist stand, where Chou En-lai of China, Jawaharlal Nehru of India, and Gamal Nasser of Egypt emerged as world leaders. Nehru and Nasser later became advocates of "non-alignment."

50 "Final Statement," in Torres and Fabella, *Emergent Gospel*, 269.

51 Torres, "Dar-es-Salaam," in Boff and Elizondo, *Convergences and Differences,* 112.

52 "Final Statement," in Torres and Fabella, *Emergent Gospel*, 269.

53 Ibid.

## CHAPTER TWO: EATWOT'S FIRST FIVE YEARS

1 Another means was through its bulletin, *Voices from the Third World*, first published in Dec., 1978, under the title *Voices of the Third World*. As some members rejected this title as presumptuous and triumphalist, it was changed starting with the June 1980 issue.

2 See Torres, "Opening Address," in Appiah-Kubi and Torres, *African Theology*, 5-7. The book contains the main papers from this conference.

3 Not all women invited to EATWOT conferences are necessarily members of the Association, but they generally accept EATWOT's liberation orientation.

4 Mercy Amba Oduyoye, "The Value of African Religious Beliefs and Practices for Christian Theology," in Appiah-Kubi and Torres, *African Theology*, 112.

5 See Rose Zoe-Obianga, "The Role of Women in Present-Day Africa," and Constance Baratang Thetele, "Women in South Africa: The WAAIC," in Appiah-Kubi and Torres, *African Theology*, 145-149 and 150-154.

6 The process and main contents of the conference, as well as some

post-conference assessments, are contained in Virginia Fabella, ed., *Asia's Struggle for Full Humanity: Towards a Relevant Theology* (Maryknoll, N.Y.: Orbis Books, 1980). The preparation for the conference began the year before with the formation of national working groups. The task of these groups as well as the preparations in India, the Philippines, and Sri Lanka are found on pp. 7-9.

7 For her full paper, see Henriette (Marianne) Katoppo, "Asian Theology: An Asian Woman's Perspective," in Fabella, *Asia's Struggle*, 140-151. This paper was the basis of her book, *Compassionate and Free*.

8 In particular, the tension brought about by the report on the "live-in" with militant Tamils given from a Tamil perspective. This was objected to by the Singhalese at the conference as one-sided.

9 Aloysius Pieris, "Towards an Asian Theology of Liberation: Some Religio-Cultural Guidelines," in Fabella, *Asia's Struggle*, 75-76.

10 The two positions are described in more detail in Fabella, *Asia's Struggle*, 11; also in *Voices 2* (June 1979): 19-28 and *Voices 7* (December 1984): 9.

11 "The Final Statement" in Fabella, *Asia's Struggle*, 155. See pp. 152-160 for the entire statement.

12 The main documents of this conference are published in Torres and Eagleson, *Christian Communities*.

13 "Final Statement," in Torres and Eagleson, *Christian Communities*, 244. The statement on women is on p. 245.

14 See ibid., 245.

15 The only substantial contribution by a woman in *Basic Christian Communities* was actually the final document of a pre-conference seminar with an introduction by Cora Ferro. "Surprising as it may sound," writes Ferro, "it was the first time that Christian women had gotten together to reflect systematically on the situation of women in Latin America." Ferro, "The Latin American Woman: The Praxis and Theology of Liberation" (p. 24). The final document itself admits the "absence of any theological reflection that incorporates the women's question," and urges every theologian of liberation to "reformulate his or her theological categories from a women's standpoint" (pp. 33, 36).

16 The major documents of the conference and related material are found in Fabella and Torres, *Irruption*. The verb 'to irrupt' (not to be confused with 'erupt') is defined "to intrude suddenly or with force"; its noun form 'irruption' means "a breaking or bursting in." See *The Random House Dictionary of the English Language* (unabridged ed.) (N.Y.: Random House, 1973). The final statement uses the term to designate the "irruption of exploited classes, marginalized cultures, and dominated races . . . bursting from the underside of history into the world long dominated by the West. . .It is an irruption of all those who struggle for full humanity and for their rightful place in history." Fabella and Torres, *Irruption*, 195.

17 In Fabella and Torres, *Irruption*, 113-139.

18 Ibid., 113. Pieris also underlined the Western bias in contemporary

theology of religions and revolutionary theories (particularly Marxism). Both are being uncritically accepted by many Third World theologians—the very ones who decry the imposition of Western norms and values in theology and society. Pieris claims that the current theology of religions available so far is from a Western point of view and needs to be rewritten from a Third World perspective.

19 See "Preface," in Fabella and Torres, *Irruption*, xiv.

20 Engelbert Mveng, "Third World Theology—What Theology? What Third World? Evaluation by an African Delegate," in Fabella and Torres, *Irruption*, 220.

21 See (Mercy) Amba Oduyoye, "Reflections from a Third World Woman's Perspective: Women's Experience and Liberation Theologies," in Fabella and Torres, *Irruption*, 246-255, especially pp. 247-249.

22 See "Final Statement," in Fabella and Torres, *Irruption*, especially pp. 193, 200, and 205.

23 Elected were Emilio Carvalho (Angola) as president, Sergio Torres (Chile) as vice-president, Virginia Fabella (Philippines) as secretary, Engelbert Mveng (Cameroun) as African coordinator, Tissa Balasuriya (Sri Lanka) as Asian coordinator, Julio de Santa Ana (Uruguay) as Latin American coordinator, and James Cone as U.S. Minorities coordinator.

24 From an unpublished paper: "Proposal for the Future of EATWOT." Delhi Conference (First Five-year Term), EATWOT Archives.

25 Ibid.

26 These elements are culled from the final statement of the Delhi conference. See Fabella and Torres, *Irruption*, 198-201.

27 See ibid., 196, 199-202, 204.

28 The EATWOT women's acceptance of these common assumptions and convictions only becomes obvious in their future theological contribution, though nuanced differently on each continent. While agreeing with the EATWOT basic principles, the women later enlarge on the EATWOT methodology as well.

29 Oduyoye, "Reflections," in Fabella and Torres, *Irruption*, 247.

30 Ibid.

31 Ibid., 247.

## CHAPTER TREE: THE EATWOT WOMEN'S COMMISSION

1 The main papers related to this conference are found in Virginia Fabella and Sergio Torres, eds. *Doing Theology in a Divided World* (Maryknoll, N.Y.: Orbis Books, 1985).

2 Africa was represented by Mercy Amba Oduyoye (Ghana/ Nigeria) and Rose Zoe-Obianga (Cameroun); Asia by Mary John Mananzan (Philippines), Marianne Katoppo (Indonesia), and Soon Kyung Park (Korea); Latin America by Carmen Lora (Peru), Ivone Gebara (Brazil), and Elsa Tamez (Mexico/Costa Rica). Sun Ai Lee Park came as an observer representing the

Asian women's theological journal, *In God's Image*, while I was part of the conference *ex officio*, being EATWOT's executive secretary at the time.

3 See Torres, "Opening Address," in Torres and Fabella, *Emergent Gospel*, 5; also Torres, "Opening Address," in Appiah-Kubi and Torres, *African Theology*, 9.

4 "Doing Theology in a Divided World: Final Statement of the Sixth EATWOT Conference," in Fabella and Torres, *Doing Theology*, 179.

5 Torres, "Preface," in Fabella and Torres, *Doing Theology*, xiii.

6 With such diversity, reactions to the dialogue ranged from excitement to frustration and disappointment. See Torres, "Preface," in Fabella and Torres, *Doing Theology*, xi-xiii; and assessments by Tissa Balasuriya, "A Third World Perspective," and by Letty Russell, "A First World Perspective," in Fabella and Torres, *Doing Theology*, 197-211.

7 See "Final Statement" in Fabella and Torres, *Doing Theology*, 192-193.

8 See Russell, "A First World Perspective," in Fabella and Torres, *Doing Theology*, 209-210; also Lee Cormie, "Report on EATWOT Conference," *The Ecumenist* 21 (May-June 1983), 76.

9 See Rosemary Radford Ruether, "A Feminist Perspective," in Fabella and Torres, *Doing Theology*, 65-71.

10 The foregoing observations on sexism are contained in the final statement. See Fabella and Torres, *Doing Theology*, 186-187.

11 Russell, "A First World Perspective," in Fabella and Torres, *Doing Theology*, 209.

12 "Final Statement," in Fabella and Torres, *Doing Theology*, 186. One of the practical conclusions of the session with the First and Third World women was the consensus to continue the dialogue in an organized way through EATWOT. Plans for this joint meeting are under way.

13 Torres, then EATWOT vice-president, saw the "power of the women theologians" in Geneva, stating that their number and quality made the dialogue a real challenge to the sexist interpretation of theology. See "Preface," in Fabella and Torres, *Doing Theology*, xv-xvi.

14 "Final Statement," in Fabella and Torres, *Doing Theology*, 187.

15 Ibid., 193.

16 Henceforth to be referred to as the Women's Commission, or simply, the Commission. The EATWOT women carefully avoided using the word "feminist" in the title of their commission. In many Third World countries, the term had a negative connotation as something Western, too liberal, and anti-men.

17 The EATWOT Constitution names the executive secretary as ultimately responsible for the entire EATWOT program, which includes the work of commissions. As I held that position from 1981 to 1986, I had to coordinate as well as supervise the Commission's program by myself until I could find a program coordinator to assist me. Mary John Mananzan from the Philippines assumed this important role from June 1985 to December 1986.

18 Tamez later asked that Latin America be divided into five areas with

a separate coordinator for each, the areas being Central America (which she would coordinate), Brazil, the Andean region, the Southern Cone, and the Caribbean region.

19 See Elsa Tamez, *"Informe de la reunion de teologia latinoamericana desde la perspective de la mujer."* Report submitted to members of the EATWOT executive committee. Women's Commission (Second Five-year Term), EATWOT Archives.

20 See Tamez, *"Informe,"* 1-2.

21 "Theology from the Perspective of Women. Final Statement: Latin American Conference, Buenos Aires, Argentina, Oct. 30-Nov. 3, 1985," in Tamez, *Through Her Eyes*, 151. This volume contains selected essays from the consultation.

22 Delores S. Williams, "Foreword," in Tamez, *Through Her Eyes*, vii.

23 See Ivone Gebara, "Women Doing Theology in Latin America," in Tamez, *Through Her Eyes*, 39-40.

24 Elsa Tamez, "Introduction: The Power of the Naked," in Tamez, *Through Her Eyes*, 5.

25 See ibid., 4-5.

26 Ibid., 6.

27 Ibid., 10.

28 "Final Statement," in Tamez, *Through Her Eyes*, 152.

29 Ibid., 151.

30 A number of position papers dealt with violence against women, discrimination in the workplace, women's inferior status in the church and their difficulties as church women, and the theological roots of discrimination against women. These papers are found in Elsa Tamez, ed. *El rostro femenino de la teologia* (San Jose, Costa Rica: DEI, 1986). For the English translation of the theological roots of women's oppression, see Maria Clara Bingemer, "Reflections on the Trinity," in *Through Her Eyes*, 57-61.

31 "Final Statement," in Tamez, *Through Her Eyes*, 151.

32 Tamez, "Introduction," in Tamez, *Through Her Eyes*, 8.

33 "Final Statement," in *Through Her Eyes*, 152-153.

34 For the five specific goals of the meeting as well as the steps in the preparation, see Women's Commission (Second Five-year Term), EATWOT Archives.

35 Since only white women attended the national meeting in New Zealand, they chose not to participate in the Asian consultation but to join the inter-world dialogue originally scheduled for 1987.

36 The number includes observers and representatives from EATWOT.

37 According to *Pro Mundi Vita* Asia-Australasia dossier No. 39, "this conference had a unique significance for the development of the women's movement in the Church of Asia. There have been other conferences before this one, but they were organized either on limited regional or denominational lines. The Manila conference was the first pan-Asian and ecumenical conference of its kind." Editor's note in "Feminine Voices in Asian Theology:

Selected Papers from the Asian Women's Consultation, Manila, 21-30 November 1985," *Pro Mundi Vita* 4/1986, 1.

[38] "Final Statement: Asian Church Women Speak," in Fabella and Lee Park, *Dare to Dream*, 148. The book was first jointly published in Hong Kong in 1989 by the Asian Women's Resource Centre for Culture and Theology and the Asian Office of the Women's Commission of EATWOT.

[39] The theological papers, except those written by the Malaysian delegates which were omitted per their request, are reproduced in "Proceedings: Asian Women's Consultation," Manila, November 21-30, 1985. Only three of the biblical reflections are included in the Proceedings (pp. 50-72), as the other reflections were not related to the national situation as prescribed.

[40] For an account regarding the composite paper, see "Proceedings," 15-17. "The process turned out to be in itself a study of how women of different backgrounds, experiences and ages can work together to create and give birth to something new" (p. 17). For a summary of the evaluations, see Appendix K (pp. 206-208). To quote one participant: "The struggle we went through together was very positive and crucial to women's struggle for liberation. I feel very much a participant in this struggle. I feel challenged and affirmed as a woman, an Asian woman" (p. 17). For a sampling of the composite papers, see Appendices C to H (pp. 73-205). The method of composite papers has since been used in preparing for other EATWOT conferences in Asia.

[41] "Final Statement," in Fabella and Lee Park, *Dare to Dream*, 149.

[42] See ibid.

[43] See ibid., 149-150.

[44] Ibid., 150.

[45] Because the executive committee was scheduled to meet in Cairo after the joint meeting, I suggested using this occasion to organize the intercontinental conference to be held in 1986, and consequently invited Mananzan, as program coordinator, and the three continental coordinators for a planning session prior to the African meeting. As it turned out, only Mananzan, besides myself, could attend, so the planning session was cancelled.

[46] The proceedings and main papers of this consultation are found in *"Rapport General: Consultation pour 'Afrique Francophone,"* Yaounde, Cameroun, August 3-9, 1986. Bound mimeographed. Some of the papers as well as the conference recommendations have been translated into English and published in Fabella and Oduyoye, *Passion and Compassion*.

[47] Some of the presentations and the conference statement, including papers which have been combined and edited, appear in Fabella and Oduyoye, *Passion and Compassion*. For other documents related to this meeting, see Women's Commission (Second Five-year Term), EATWOT Archives.

[48] *"Rapport General,"* 115.

[49] "Final Statement," in Fabella and Oduyoye, *Passion and Compas-*

*sion,* 61.

[50] Ibid., 64.

[51] Ibid., 64-65.

[52] Ibid., 65.

[53] Ibid.

[54] Quoting Lee Park in the introduction of "Proceedings," 4.

## CHAPTER FOUR: THE "OAXTEPEC ENCOUNTER" AND AFTER

[1] The planning meeting was attended by Mananzan as program coordinator, myself as executive secretary and liaison to the Women's Commission, and Park, Tamez, and Oduyoye representing Asia, Latin America, and Africa respectively. Mananzan, Oduyoye, and I were also in the assembly preparatory committee.

[2] "Final Document," in Fabella and Oduyoye, *Passion and Compassion,* 184. The planners chose as criteria for the conference participants: (1) participation in a national/continental consultation; (2) involvement in theological efforts; (3) commitment to women's questions and issues; and (4) perspective of the poor and oppressed.

[3] "Preparatory Committee Report," 2, International Women's Conference (Second Five-year Term), EATWOT Archives. "Women and Theology," which was to focus on methodology, was later dropped, and methodology was combined with Christology.

[4] Ibid., 1.

[5] The Working Constitution approved in 1983 only specified "continental and denominational balance" in admitting new members to EATWOT.

[6] Chosen by the executive committee, the two women were Odoyuye and Mananzan as African and Asian representative respectively, while the two men were Julio de Santa Ana as Latin American representative, and Virgil Elizondo as U.S. Minorities representative. As executive secretary, I was an ex-officio member of the preparatory committee for the assembly, together with Dussel, chairperson of the local support committee.

[7] Compared to less than five per cent at the founding assembly in 1976, and barely twenty-four per cent at the first general assembly in 1981.

[8] This is the title of the book containing the original papers prepared for the women's intercontinental conference. See Virginia Fabella and Dolorita Martinez, eds., *The Oaxtepec Encounter* (Ecumenical Association of Third World Theologians, n.d.).

[9] "Final Document" in Fabella and Oduyoye, *Passion and Compassion,* 185.

[10] Unfortunately there is no written version of Tamez's talk.

[11] Israel's united action for justice was actually on behalf of the master whose property, the concubine, was violated, ignoring the atrocity done to the woman herself. Phyllis Trible suggests a rereading of Judges 19:30, 20:7, enjoining the reader/listener "to consider *her,* take counsel, and speak out"

(emphasis mine). Phyllis Trible, *Texts of Terror* (Philadelphia: Fortress Press, 1984), 86. Trible explains that since there is no neuter pronoun in Hebrew, this is a permissible translation, but "to speak for this woman is to interpret against the narrator, plot, other characters, and the biblical tradition because they have shown her neither compassion nor attention." Ibid.

[12] Circles or associations of women in theology are examples. They affirm the EATWOT women's assertion that "among the efforts being made toward liberation from oppression, theologizing emerges as a specific manner in which women struggle for their right to life." "Final Document" in Fabella and Oduyoye, *Passion and Compassion*, 186.

[13] "Final Document," in Fabella and Oduyoye, *Passion and Compassion*, 186. The next four quotes are from the same page of the final document.

[14] See "Introduction," in Fabella and Oduyoye, *Passion and Compassion*, xii.

[15] "Final Document" in Fabella and Oduyoye, *Passion and Compassion*," 186.

[16] Ibid., 187. The next two quotes are also taken from the same page of the final document.

[17] Ibid., 187-188.

[18] Ibid., 188.

[19] See ibid., 188, also xiv.

[20] See Ana Maria Tepedino, "Feminist Theology as the Fruit of Passion and Compassion," in Fabella and Oduyoye, *Passion and Compassion*, 165-172. Her article gave the book its title.

[21] See "Final Document," in Fabella and Oduyoye, *Passion and Compassion*, 188.

[22] See ibid., 186.

[23] "Introduction" in Fabella and Oduyoye, *Passion and Compassion*, xi.

[24] See Virginia Fabella, "A Common Methodology for Diverse Christologies?" in Fabella and Oduyoye, *Passion and Compassion*, 117.

[25] "Final Document," in Fabella and Oduyoye, *Passion and Compassion*, 190. The passage was excerpted from the biblical reflection given by Ana Maria Tepedino as part of the closing liturgy.

[26] See ibid.

[27] Maria Clara Lucchetti Bingemer, "Preface—Third World Theologies: Conversion to Others," in *Third World Theologies: Commonalities and Divergences*, ed. K. C. Abraham (Maryknoll, N.Y.: Orbis Books, 1990), vii.

[28] Ibid., viii.

[29] See chap. 1 above.

[30] See "Commonalities, Divergences, and Cross-fertilization among Third World Theologies," in Abraham, *Third World Theologies*, 196. This document based on the EATWOT conference/assembly in Oaxtepec is not an official statement since it was not completed on time to get the assembly's approval. Nevertheless, it will henceforth be referred to as "the Oaxtepec

document."

[31] "The almost uniform conclusion of the Decade's research is that, with few exceptions, women's relative access to economic resources, incomes, and employment has worsened, their burdens of work have increased, and their relative and even absolute health, nutritional and educational status has declined." DAWN, *Development Crisis and Alternative Visions. Third World Women's Perspectives* (Bergen, Norway: Christian Michelson Institute, 1985), 21; quoted in Vandana Shiva, "Development as a New Project of Western Patriarchy," in *Reweaving the World: The Emergence of Ecofeminism*, ed. Irene Diamond and Gloria Feman Orenstein (San Francisco: Sierra Club Books, 1990), 191.

[32] See "Commonalities, Divergences, and Cross-fertilization," in Abraham, *Third World Theologies*, 196.

[33] The three elements are culled from Bingemer, "Conversion to Others," in Abraham, *Third World Theologies*, viii-ix.

[34] Ibid., viii-ix.

[35] See "Commonalities, Divergences, and Cross-fertilization," in Abraham, *Third World Theologies*, 199.

[36] See ibid., 206. Similar questions are taken up by Asian EATWOT women in their subsequent writings and gatherings. See, for example, Virginia Fabella, "Christology from an Asian Woman's Perspective" in Fabella and Lee Park, *Dare to Dream*, 8-9. Also, Cynthia R. Chapman, "A Comparison of Gordon Kaufman's Christology with Those of Asian Feminists," *Ching Feng* 34 (September 1991): 154-167.

[37] During the conference, new officers were elected: Sergio Torres (Chile) as president; K. C. Abraham (India) as vicepresident; Teresa Okure (Nigeria) as secretary; Simon Mimela (South Africa) as African coordiantor; Virginia Fabella (Philippines) as Asian coordinator; Maria Clara Bingemer (Brazil) as Latin Amertican coordinator; and Virgil Elizondo (United States) as U.S. Minorities coordinator.

[38] What to the Executive Committee was construed as an "advance" for the Association, i.e. the suspension of the position of an over-all coordinator for the Women's Commission, had a negative result for the Commission. See chap. 5, p. 81 below.

[39] See "Women's Evaluation of EATWOT" in *Third World Theologies*, 143-146. For another assessment, see Mercy Amba Oduyoye's unpublished report, "Women's Critique of EATWOT: The African Continent," also written for the assembly. Oaxtepec Conference (Second Five-year Term), EATWOT Archives. Through some miscommunication, Oduyoye's report was not incorporated in the women's evaluation.

[40] "Commonalities, Differences, and Cross-fertilization," in Abraham, *Third World Theologies*, 208-209.

[41] "Final Communique: Consultation between Third World Women in Third World Contexts and Third World Women in First World Contexts." Unpublished paper marked "Not for public distribution."

[42] See Virginia Fabella, Peter K.H. Lee, and David Kwang-sun Suh, eds., *Asian Christian Spirituality: Reclaiming Traditions* (Maryknoll. N.Y.: Orbis Books, 1992).

[43] See ibid., 8.

[44] See Mercy Amba Oduyoye and Musimbi Kanyoro, *Talitha, kumi! Proceedings of the Convocation of African Women Theologians* (Ibadan, Nigeria: Daystar Press, 1990), 5. The Circle of Concerned African Women Theologians will sometimes be referred to in this paper as "the Circle."

[45] Ibid., 19.

[46] Ibid., 1. The Institute has chosen to focus on the Islamic, Christian, and African indigenous religious tradition, a triple religious heritage that has been interwoven into the culture, affecting the entire continent.

[47] Local Circles are encouraged to create network circles and to conduct studies in African languages to enable women who do not use European languages to participate. See Oduyoye and Kanyoro, *Talitha Kumi!*, 3. "We shall have fewer problems with our language about God and in our human relations if we use African languages." Ibid., 15. The International Planning Committee itself worked in English, French and Swahili (see p. 9).

[48] Ibid., 184.

[49] Ibid., 12-13.

[50] See ibid., 13.

[51] Ibid., 12. Accounts of "women's violence against other women" kept recurring during the Institute. In the treatment of widows, for example, it is the women of the family and sisters-in-law who subject the widow to dehumanizing widowhood rites and practices. See pp. 189-190.

[52] The women, however, realized there was still much work to be done. See ibid., 11-14, 19-25, 182-209. See also AMKA, Issue No. 1 (an occasional newsletter of the Biennial Institute of African Women in Religion and Culture), c. 1991. The newsletter is produced by the Circle, with each region taking turns in its publication.

[53] Fourteen of these essays are published in Oduyoye and Kanyoro, *The Will to Arise*.

[54] Marie-Bernadette Mbuy-Beya, "Woman's Word on Woman's Work," 8-9. Unpublished report on the Women's Commission in Africa prepared for the EATWOT general assembly in 1992. Translated from French by Brother David P. Mahoney, C.F.X.

[55] Ibid., 9. The two quotes that follow are from the same page.

[56] See ibid. The report also admitted the difficulty of ecumenical dialogue among women in communities still in search of their identity, as in Zaire.

[57] Ibid., 10.

[58] Ibid., 12.

[59] The interviews with the women were edited by Tamez and published under the title, *Las mujeres toman la palabra* (San Jose, Costa Rica: Departamento Ecumenico de Investigaciones, 1989). The interviews with

the male liberation theologians, also conducted by Tamez, were first published in Spanish and later translated into English under the title *Against Machismo* (Oak Park, Ill.: Meyer Stone Books, 1987).

60 Tamez, *"Presentacion,"* chap. in *Las mujeres*, 10-11.

61 For the report on the Singapore meeting, see *Asian Women Doing Theology* (Hong Kong: Asian Women's Resource Centre for Culture and Theology, 1989).

62 ATC III is the acronym for the third Asian Theological Conference. As a quinquennial EATWOT event in Asia, the first ATC took place in Sri Lanka in 1979, while the second, ATC II, was held in Hong Kong in 1984. See chap. 2, pp. 46-49 for an overview of ATC I.

63 The Philippine paper also contains future tasks for Filipino women theologians. See "In Search of a Filipino Women's Hermeneutical Principle," *Pintig Diwa Faculty Journal* 10 (October 1989): 1-12. The journal is published by the faculty of St. Scholastica's College in Manila.

64 Gnanadason, Lee Park as Asian coordinator of the Women's Commission, and myself, as the EATWOT regional coordinator for Asia.

65 The Malaysian paper entitled "Roots of Patriarchy in Asia" used Gerda Lerner's analysis of the origins of patriarchy in *The Creation of Patriarchy* (New York: Oxford University Press, 1986), 15-53.

66 See unpublished draft prepared for the Madras consultation by Kwok Pui-lan entitled "Feminist Hermeneutics from a Chinese Perspective," 8.

67 See unpublished statement of the "Asian Women Theologians' Meeting, December, 1990, Madras."

## CHAPTER FIVE: EATWOT WOMEN: THEIR OWN THEOLOGICAL JOURNEYS

1 All interviews were done between Sept. 1989 and Jan. 1991.

2 Since EATWOT women are on three continents, I was limited in my selection to those I could meet within a certain time frame without extra travel expense.

3 Other EATWOT women interviewed but only partially due to lack of time were Rosemary Edet (Nigeria), Rosemary Nthamburi (Kenya), Crescy John (India), Marianne Katoppo (Indonesia), and Chung Hyun Kyung (Korea).

4 Mercy Amba Oduyoye, interview by author, Geneva, Switzerland, Oct. 3, 1989, tape recording. Unless otherwise indicated, all quotes in this entire chapter are from the interviews.

5 Juan Luis Segundo, *The Liberation of Theology* (Maryknoll, N.Y.: Orbis Books, 1976).

6 Oduyoye confessed, however, that she took exception to the mysogynist language of the African folktales recounted by a male member of the African delegation, mostly to entertain.

7 A revised version of Oduyoye's Selly Oaks lecture is entitled "Feminism: A Precondition for a Christian Anthropology," chap. in Oduyoye,

*Hearing and Knowing*, 120-137.

8 Oduyoye claims that the liberating dimensions in African tradition have been eroded by the Western system, such dimensions as the custom of choosing women as rulers and of women owning land.

9 See Oduyoye, "Trinity and Community," chap. in *Hearing and Knowing*, 138-145.

10 See chap. 4, pp.58-60 above.

11 See Mercy Amba Oduyoye, "A Biennial Institute of African Women in Religion and Culture," *AMKA* 1 (1991), 9.

12 Teresa Okure, interview by author, Amsterdam, Netherlands, Sept. 29, 1989, tape recording.

13 Okure explained that they had a professor whose over-zealous approach to the women issue succeeded in alienating people. "But if she hadn't been there to introduce that program, I probably wouldn't have been consciously aware then of the women issue in theology."

14 See Teresa Okure, "Biblical Perspectives on Women: Eve, the Mother of All," *Voices from the Third World* (Philippine edition) 8 (December 1985): 17-24.

15 See Okure, "Epilogue: The Will to Arise: Reflections on Luke 8:40-56," in Oduyoye and Kanyoro, *The Will to Arise*, 221-230. The title of the book is derived from her paper.

16 Okure admits that the secular world is ahead of the Church in recognizing the oppression of women. For most Catholic women, including Sisters, it is still "if Rome has spoken, then that is it."

17 Maria Clara Bingemer, interview by author, Amsterdam, Netherlands, Sept. 30, 1989, tape recording.

18 In this section on Latin American women, the title "liberation theology" refers to Latin American liberation theology, unless stipulated otherwise.

19 A step preliminary to basic Christian communities in which people gather to read the Gospel together and reflect on its meaning for their lives.

20 This "job" ranges from listening and "accompanying" to helping church groups reflect and then articulate their aspirations and make their own choices and decisions.

21 Maria Clara Bingemer, "Women in the Future of Liberation Theology," in *Expanding the View: Gustavo Gutierrez and the Future of Liberation Theology*, ed. Marc H. Ellis and Otto Maduro (Maryknoll, N.Y.: Orbis Books, 1990), 174. This lack had been detected as early as 1980. See chap. 2 above. See also Torres and Eagleson, *Christian Communities*, especially 4-5, 24-56, 234.

22 Bingemer notes that Latin American women find the terms "feminist" and "feminine" ambiguous and prefer to use the expression "from the optic (view) of women."

23 See Maria Clara (Lucchetti) Bingemer, "Reflections on the Trinity," in Tamez, *Through Her Eyes*, 56-80.

[24] See Maria Clara (Lucchetti) Bingemer, "Jesus Christ and the Salvation of Women," in Fabella and Martinez, *Oaxtepec Encounter*, 194-204.

[25] As a collective work, see Ivone Gebara and Maria Clara Bingemer, *Mary Mother of God, Mother of the Poor* (Maryknoll, N.Y.: Orbis Books, 1989). Gebara is also an EATWOT member.

[26] Elsa Tamez, interview by author, Geneva, Switzerland, October 4, 1989, tape recording.

[27] Tamez also studied literature and linguistics at the national university in Costa Rica.

[28] Elsa Tamez, *Bible of the Oppressed* (Maryknoll, N.Y.: Orbis Books, 1982), originally published in Spanish in 1979.

[29] Tamez noted, for example, that in Jas 2:15, both "brother" and "sister" are used. This is surprising since James, like the other Scripture writers, does not generally employ inclusive language. This has led Tamez to conclude that there were probably many poor women in the community or communities James was addressing.

[30] See Elsa Tamez, "The Woman Who Complicated the History of Salvation," in Pobee and Von Wartenberg-Potter, *New Eyes*, 5-17.

[31] Tamez's thesis was published under the title *Contra toda condena. La justificacion por la fe desde los excluidos* (San Jose, Costa Rica: DEI, 1991).

[32] Tamez posits that in accepting the gift of God's justice, the "non-persons," the "excluded" in society, are converted into creative subjects capable of transforming the very history that excludes and kills. In this sense, justification by faith (and not by the law) is the historical starting point of the revelation of God's justice.

[33] Mary John Mananzan, interview by author, Manila, Philippines, Nov. 12, 1989, tape recording.

[34] Mary John Mananzan, "Theological Perspectives of a Religious Woman Today, " in *The Future of Liberation Theology*, ed. Marc Ellis and Otto Maduro (Maryknoll, N.Y.: Orbis Books, 1989), 421. It recounts her involvement in different people's movements as well as the resulting anguish that comes with such a commitment.

[35] When asked whether she was influenced by Latin American liberation theologians, Mananzan confessed that her theological training had been very German. "We never read anything except German theologians. I didn't get in contact with Latin American liberation theologians until much later."

[36] Mary John Mananzan, "Emerging Spirituality Among Religious in the Philippines," in *Prophets for the Third Millennium*, First Religious Life Week (Quezon City, Philippines: Claretian Publications, 1990), 143.

[37] Later edited and combined with another article on the same topic. See Mary John Mananzan and Sun Ai (Lee) Park, "Emerging Spirituality of Asian Women," in Fabella and Oduyoye, *Passion and Compassion*, 77-88.

[38] See footnote no. 34 above.

[39] Like Mananzan, most of the EATWOT women regretted the executive committee's decision not to appoint a program coordinator for the term

1986-1991.  They felt not only that the momemtum of their corporate progress was lost but that the rest of the women's program was left dangling.

40 Aruna Gnanadason, interview by author, Madras, India, Dec. 21, 1990, tape recording.

41 For the report on the meeting, see Aruna Gnanadason, ed., *Towards a Theology of Humanhood: Women's Perspectives* (Delhi, India: I.S.P.C.K. for All India Council of Christian Women, 1986).

42 Elisabeth Schussler Fiorenza, *In Memory of Her: A Feminist Reconstruction of Christian Origins* (New York: Crossroad, 1983).

43 Rosemary Radford Ruether, *Sexism and God-Talk: Toward a Feminist Theology* (Philadelphia: The Westminister Press, 1987).

44 Kwok Pui-lan, interview by author, Madras, India, Dec. 17, 1990. Tape recording.

45 Kwok was at the diocesan synod that discussed the ordination of women.  A hot debate arose around marriage and children.  Kwok recalled thinking: "It is not a problem for men; why should it be a problem for women?"

46 Kwok Pui-lan, "Mothers and Daughters, Writers and Fighters," in Russell and others, *Our Mothers' Gardens*, 29.

47 See Kwok Pui-lan, "Discovering the Bible in the Non-Biblical World," *Semeia* 47 (1989): 25-42.

48 Sun Ai Lee Park, interview by author, Kuala Lumpur, Malaysia, Nov. 1, 1989, tape recording.

49 See chap. 1, p. 11. above,

50 Sun Ai Lee Park, untitled manuscript [photocopy], 1-2.

51 See *In God's Image*, 185/12/86 (September 1987), front cover.

52 Sun Ai Lee Park, "Envisioning a Future Church as an Asian Woman," *Voices from the Third World* 12 (June 1989): 64-94.

53 Lee Park to Fabella, undated handwritten letter received in June, 1991.

## CHAPTER SIX: EATWOT WOMEN EN ROUTE

1 All quotes in the first three paragraphs are from the taped interviews used in chap. 5. With regard to being a "select" group, it is well to caution the reader that EATWOT women represent but a small portion of women theologians on their own continents.

2 See chap. 2, pp.22, 29-30 above.

3 See "Final Document" in Fabella and Oduyoye, *Passion and Compassion*, 184-190.  Some of the commonalities and differences are noted in chap. 4 above.

4 See chap. 2, pp. 27-28 above.

5 The reader is reminded that the Third World women who participated in the Commission's program were not necessarily EATWOT members. Moreover, corporate development does not imply uniform development.

6 While EATWOT women agree to do theology "from the perspective

of Third World women," they may not all interpret "women's perspective" in the same way. For example, see chap. 4, pp. 60-61 above. In this work, however, I use it in the sense indicated in this paragraph.

7 This pattern of growth is actually reflective of my own.

8 See Tamez's remark about herself and other Latin American women, pp. 77-79 above.

9 Conversation with Kwok, Stony Point, New York, Nov. 22, 1991. It must be recalled that many people had fled to Hong Kong precisely to escape the Communist regime in China.

10 See chap. 4, p. 58 above.

11 See Ivone Gebara, "Women Doing Theology in Latin America," in Tamez, *Through Her Eyes*, 39-40.

12 The classical theological themes such as Christology, soteriology, ecclesiology, and so forth.

13 There are some exceptions. In Asia, for example, Filipino women are developing a theology of struggle together with their male colleagues. In Africa, some women see the need for "complementarity," that is, "women should theologize alongside men . . . complementing what men have done so it is balanced." Rosemary Edet, interview by author, Harare, Zimbabwe, Jan. 12, 1991.

14 Interview with Chung Hyun Kyung, Maryknoll, N.Y., Aug. 4, 1991. There is, however, another view regarding minjung women's theology. According to the Korean women's report for the Madras meeting in 1990, there is "a strong move to develop a minjung women's theology using the hermeneutical principles or methodology of minjung theology." "The Critical Hermeneutical Principles of Korean Women Theologians," 16. Unpublished paper.

15 Oduyoye, "Women's Critique of EATWOT: The African Continent," 9. Unpublished paper prepared for the EATWOT assembly in Oaxtepec.

16 Ibid., 8.

17 Interview with Oduyoye, Oct. 3, 1989. Oduyoye says that patriarchy exists in Africa, but is not named as such. Hence the term does not have negative overtones. It would be interesting to study whether the form of male domination existing in pre-colonized Africa (or in pre-colonized Asia or Latin America for that matter) can really be classified as "patriarchy" in the Western sense.

18 In their final document in Oaxtepec, the women affirmed "the need to contextualize our Christology in the oppressed and painful realities of our continents." Fabella and Oduyoye, *Passion and Compassion*, 187-188. Differences due to context are noted on p. 188.

19 See Oduyoye and Kanyoro, *Talitha, kumi!*, 106-212 passim.

20 See Therese Souga, "The Christ-Event from the Viewpoint of African Women: A Catholic Perspective," in Fabella and Oduyoye, *Passion and Compassion*, 27.

21 See Elizabeth Amoah and Mercy Amba Oduyoye, "The Christ for

African Women," in Fabella and Oduyoye, *Passion and Compassion*, 43-45.

[22] Bingemer, "Jesus Christ and the Salvation of Women," in Fabella and Martinez, *The Oaxtepec Encounter*, 194-204; see also Nelly Ritchie, "Women and Christology," in Tamez, *Through Her Eyes*, 81-95.

[23] Discussion by Kwok, Mananzan and Fabella on Christology from an Asian women's perspective, Hong Kong, Jan. 30, 1991. The three women agree that the image of Christ as the Suffering Servant or self-emptying Christ which is popular among Asian Christian women has served to promote the existing overemphasis on women's self-denial. Instead of a Christology of kenosis, the women suggest a Christology of Pentecost, to respond to the need of Asian women for authentic appreciation of self rather than further self-effacement. For a parallel African position, see Louise Tappa, "The Christ-Event from the Viewpoint of African Women: A Protestant Perspective," in Fabella and Oduyoye, *Passion and Compassion*, 33.

[24] EATWOT women are aware, however, that this is a problem for some Christian feminists in the West. See, for example, Bingemer, "Jesus Christ and the Salvation of Women," in Fabella and Martinez, *Oaxtepec Encounter*, 194-195.

[25] Amoah and Oduyoye, "The Christ for African Women," in Fabella and Oduyoye, *Passion and Compassion*, 44.

[26] Bingemer, "Jesus Christ and the Salvation of Women," in Fabella and Martinez, *Oaxtepec Encounter*, 202.

[27] Park Soon Kyung, EATWOT member, quoted in Choi Man Ja, "Feminist Christology," in *Asian Women Doing Theology*, 177.

[28] Discussion on Christology from Asian women's perspective, Jan. 30, 1991. This viewpoint is reflected in Oriental art where humans are portrayed as tiny, almost invisible creatures before the grandeur and vastness of nature around them.

[29] Most of the more recent comers to EATWOT use "feminist" unhesitatingly, while others are still uncomfortable with the term. In this section, "feminist" is used if the interviewee herself used the term.

[30] The influence of books deserves notice. Some younger women members of EATWOT claim that their interest in joining EATWOT and in doing theology from a Third World women's perspective had been sparked by EATWOT books such as *With Passion and Compassion*.

[31] For an example of the difference in approach and interpretation of women from the same continent doing theology collectively, see chap. 4, pp. 61-63.

[32] See chap. 1, p. 17 above.

[33] In the past, however, the evils of colonialism and neocolonialism were depicted mostly in economic and political terms, but seldom as a racial issue. As an example: for many years, Filipinos were condescendingly called "little brown brothers" by their American colonizers, a term which is also racist and sexist but which was not recognized as such.

[34] It was only recently that Filipino women, for instance, started

naming their multiple oppression in terms of class, gender, and race, (the last mentioned referring to their domination by a Western—and therefore white—power).

35 See in particular the Indian women's report for the Madras meeting, December 1990: "Breaking the Silence." Unpublished paper.

36 "Final Statement," in Tamez, *Through Her Eyes*, 152.

37 "Asian Women Theologians' Meeting, December, 1990, Madras," 4. Unpublished statement. Explicit reference to ecological analysis in their section on methodology is, however, absent.

38 See Shiva, "Development and Western Patriarchy," in Diamond and Feman Orenstein, *Reweaving the World*, 192-193.

39 Like many liberation theologians, both male and female, EATWOT women do not separate spirituality from theology.

40 The phrase is borrowed from Sallie McFague, *Models of God: Theology for an Ecological, Nuclear Age* (Philadelphia: Fortress Press, 1987). McFague argues for a holistic or ecological, evolutionary view of reality needed in contemporary theology, and speaks of the world as God's body.

41 See chap. 4, p. 60 above. The Latin American women insist that the study of feminist theories should be done by men and women alike.

42 For example, Delia D. Aguilar, *The Feminist Challenge: Initial Working Principles Toward Reconceptualizing the Feminist Movement in the Philippines* (Manila, Philippines: Asian Social Institute, 1988).

43 For some women, dependence on a colonizer's language, whether English, French, or Spanish, is in itself a sign of Third World-ness.

44 "Introduction," in Fabella and Oduyoye, *Passion and Compassion*, ix.

45 Important terms such as "patriarchy," "feminine," "hermeneutics," "women's perspective," and "complementarity," among others, have different shades of meaning that need to be clarified.

46 In 1989, there were over 65 major languages listed as "spoken by at least one million persons" in the Sub-Sahara region of Africa. See *The World Almanac and Book of Facts 1991* (N.Y.: World Almanac, 1990), 808-809. Swahili, spoken mostly in Kenya, Tanzania, Uganda, and Zaire, claims the largest number of speakers at 43 million. It has also been adopted as one of the working languages of the Organization of African Unity (OAU).

47 As examples, Ghana, Kenya, and Nigeria use English as one of their official languages while Zaire uses French. Cameroun lists both French and English. In 1989, English speakers numbered over 443 million in Africa; French speakers, over 121 million. See ibid.

48 This is probably the underlying reason why Latin American theologians are perceived as the "most Westernized" by Asians and Africans. Since Spanish and Portuguese are used as their main languages, Latin Americans have internalized Western culture to a greater extent than Asians and Africans.

49 This problem was posed during ATC I in 1979: can any authentic "Asian theology" be done in a Western language? See Fabella, "An Introduc-

tion," in Fabella, *Asia's Struggle*, 14.

[50] Margaret Proctor-Smith, *In Her Own Rite: Constructing Feminist Liturgical Tradition* (Nashville: Abington Press, 1990), 85; quoted in Susan Brooks Thistlethwaite, "On the Trinity," *Interpretation* 45/2 (April 1991), 159. Margaret Proctor-Smith also makes the clarifying distinction between nonsexist and inclusive language: "Nonsexist language seeks to avoid gender-specific terms. Inclusive language seeks to balance gender references." Proctor-Smith, *In Her Own Rite*, 63; quoted in ibid., 168.

[51] Tamez, for example, admits: "The name we give to God is a question that still seems strange in our (Latin American ) context. . . . In both Catholic and Protestant popular Christian communities it has occurred to no one . . . to refer to the God of the Bible as mother. And generally speaking this is still alien to Latin American feminist Christian women, or at least we do not consider it an important issue—yet." "Commentary," in Tamez, *Against Machismo*, 147.

[52] It may be for this reason—that it is not just a Western issue—that Oduyoye appeals for further work on "language about God" by EATWOT women.

[53] For example, Bingemer critiques Leonardo Boff's book on Mary, which reflects his vision of the feminine and of woman, as "totally idealistic. It's not real. It is a man's projection of what woman should be. Even if Leonardo is very sympathetic to the women's cause, he couldn't escape the machismo which is in his culture and history." Interview with Bingemer, Sept. 30, 1989. Compare Leonardo Boff, *The Maternal Face of God: The Feminine and Its Religious Expressions* (London: Collins Religious Publications, 1989), first published in Portuguese in 1979, with Gebara and Bingemer, *Mary, Mother of God*.

[54] The Latin American women present an ambivalent position. While most would agree with Tamez that "to do theology outside the framework of the theology of liberation leads nowhere" (*Against Machismo*, 141), they also recognize the need to "release ourselves from old frameworks and from categories imposed by the patriarchal system, in order to give birth to something closer to life." ("Final Statement" in Tamez, *Through Her Eyes*, 152).

[55] Interview with Chung, Aug. 4, 1991.

[56] Alida Verhoeven, "The Concept of God: A Feminine Perspective," in Tamez, *Through Her Eyes*, 54.

[57] Interview with Tamez, Oct. 4, 1989.

[58] Interview with Gnanadason, Dec. 21, 1990. See chap. 5, p. 83 above.

[59] See "Final Document," in Fabella and Oduyoye, *Passion and Compassion*, 186. See also chap. 3, p. 34 and chap. 4, p. 53 above.

[60] "The Critical Hermeneutical Principles of Korean Women Theologians," 16-17. Unpublished paper.

[61] Interview with Chung, Aug. 4, 1991.

[62] It is recognized that there is not only one Third World liberation theology or only one type of feminist theology.

[63] For the early development of womanist theology, see Delores S. Williams, "Womanist Theology: Black Women's Voices," in *Christianity and Crisis* (March 2, 1987): 66-70.

[64] See Ada-Maria Isasi-Diaz, *"Mujeristas:* A Name of Our Own," in Ellis and Maduro, *Future of Liberation Theology,* 410-419.

[65] See chap. 5 above.

[66] See especially the interview with Gutierrez in Tamez, *Against Machismo,* 39-48.

[67] See chap. 4, p. 57 above.

[68] "Breaking the Silence: Indian Women in Search of Hermeneutical Principles," 19-22. Unpublished paper.

[69] Ibid., 20.

[70] Ibid.

[71] See Fabella and Oduyoye, *Passion and Compassion,* 188.

[72] In their meetings in Manila, Seoul, and Madras, the Asian women employed dance, drama, painting and collage-making to express their reality and theology. For a Bible study they used mime at ATC III in Soeul in 1989.

[73] Chung Hyun-Kyung, "Come Holy Spirit, Renew the Whole Creation," Document No. PL 3.3, WCC Seventh Assembly, Canberra, Australia, 7-10 February, 1991, p.3. Mimeographed.

[74] K.C Abraham, "The Canberra Assembly—Some Impressions," *People's Reporter*, Feb 16-28, 1991, p. 2.

[75] In the eyes of African women, EATWOT still has to understand the different needs of EATWOT women and to extend greater assistance to the more isolated and disadvantaged among them. Oduyoye, for one, observes that "the principle of mothering in which the weakest shall receive the most attention is yet to operate in EATWOT." Oduyoye "Women's Critique of EATWOT: The African Continent," 2.

[76] As examples, the blacks and Amerindians of Latin America (Bingemer); the peoples of the non-biblical world (Kwok).

[77] See also Tissa Balasuriya, *Planetary Theology* (Maryknoll, N.Y.: Orbis Books, 1984), 152-154. However, the work as a whole is largely humanity-oriented.

[78] "Introduction," in Diamond and Orenstein, *Reweaving the World,* ix.

[79] Abraham, *Third World Theologies,* 210.

[80] As Vandana Shiva, physicist and philosopher of science active in the ecological movement in India, writes: "Justice, equality, and peace are intimately tied with ecological stability." Shiva, "Development and Western Patriarchy," in Diamond and Orenstein, *Reweaving the World,* 193.

[81] Already there was a hint of this in the Oaxtepec assembly document when it asked: "Should we not join the historical Jesus and the cosmic Christ in a rich pneumatic Christology and a cosmo-theandric vision of reality?" Abraham, *Third World Theologies,* 206-207.

## CHAPTER SEVEN: CHARTING THE FUTURE

[1] Orbis Books, which publishes works of Third World women, reports that *Mary: Mother of God, Mother of the Poor* authored by Gebara and Bingemer is selling better than any other volume in the Liberation Theology series. *With Passion and Compassion* edited by Fabella and Oduyoye will go into its fifth printing.

[2] These range from lullabies to women's prayer and confessional statements to non-verbal expressions of their dreams and struggles.

[3] The theme of the third EATWOT general assembly in Nairobi in 1992 is "A Cry for Life: The Spirituality of the Third World."

[4] See, for example, Aruna Gnanadason, "Indian Women: New Voices, New Vision," in *Third World Theologies in Dialogue: Essays in Memory of D. S. Amalorpavadass*, ed. J. Russell Chandran (Ecumenical Association of Third World Theologians, 1991), 143-151.

[5] Members of these movements should gradually be incorporated as EATWOT members. See also Samuel Rayan, "Where Do We Go from Here?" in Boff and Elizondo, *Convergences and Divergences*, 138.

[6] See chap. 6, pp. 99-103 above.

## AFTERWORD: THE JOURNEY CONTINUES

[1] The assembly took place a month after I completed the dissertation/project. Although women were only 33 percent of the total EATWOT membership at the time of the assembly, they comprised 45 percent of the Nairobi delegates. There were also 30 observers from funding agencies and other EATWOT partners.

[2] See chap. 1, p. 16 above.

[3] See chap. 1, pp. 15, 19 above.

[4] See chap. 2, pp. 27-28 above.

[5] See chap. 4, p. 54 above.

[6] With reference to the cooperative spirit, Chung Hyun Kyung remarked, "Perhaps the realization that it is not a matter of fighting among ourselves but moving together towards the same goal that makes the Nairobi conference historic." Conversation with Chung, Cambridge, Massachusetts, Oct. 30, 1992.

[7] Sergio Torres drew spontaneous applause from the women when, in his opening speech as president, he reminded his male colleagues that the women in EATWOT were their equal partners in EATWOT's theological enterprise.

[8] It was explained at the assembly that the original plan was to invite a Native American woman to give the presentation on spirituality. The major presentations as well as the women's responses will appear in a volume on the Nairobi assembly. The assembly statement was published in *Voices from the Third World* 15:1 (June 1992) : 107-140.

9 The intimate connection between land and spirituality became an important part of the assembly discussion due largely to the presentation on Spirituality by George Tinker, a Native American from the U.S.A. and the participation of Eleazar Lopez Hernandez, a Zapotecan from the Isthmus of Tehuantepec, Mexico.

10 Philippine abbreviation for "recapitulation of the previous day's activities."

11 The instructive and inspiring commentary was prepared by George Soares Prabhu of India. It was his talk on "Jesus of Faith: A Christological Contribution to an Ecumenical Christian Spirituality" that aroused in the assembly a greater interest in and appreciation of Asian religions and spirituality. Soares maintains one can be faithful to the Jesus of faith without having to give up the Buddha.

12 Cf the following conclusions and recommendations with those found in chap. 7 above.

13 The theme was subsequently changed to "Spirituality for Life: Women Struggling Against Violence." The EATWOT women also suggested that preparations for the dialogue should start at the national level and move on to the regional and interregional levels.

14 Chosen as regional coordinators of the Women's Commission were Anne Nasimiyu-Wasike for Africa, Mary John Mananzan for Asia, Tereza Cavalcanti for Latin America, and Kelly Brown-Douglas for the U.S. Minorities. At their first meeting in May, 1992, Mananzan was chosen as international coordinator.

15 The four women elected to the Executive Committee were Bernadette Mbuy-Beya (Zaire) as vice-president, Marlene Perera (Sri Lanka) as Asian coordinator, Ana Maria Tepedino (Brazil) as Latin American coordinator, and Jacqueline Grant, as coordintor of the U.S. Minorities. The other officers elected were K. C. Abraham (India) as president, Carmelo Alvarez (Costa Rica) as secretary, and Simon Maimela (South Africa) as African coordinator.

16 At a post-Nairobi conversation with EATWOT women, "Feminist Critique of Spirituality and Religion" was suggested as a possible theme for the next EATWOT assembly. A few suggested addressing indigenous culture and native wisdom from a theological perspective, or taking a serious look at post-colonialism in the Third World from the viewpoint of its worst victims. Whatever the theme, the women agreed it should challenge the present patriarchal paradigm. Said one, "It is time EATWOT faced the fact that women's issues are actually the men's problem. EATWOT should start speaking with a self-critical voice."

# SOURCES CONSULTED
◆◆◆

I. Books and Articles

Abraham, K. C., ed. *Third World Theologies: Commonalities and Divergences*. Maryknoll, N.Y.: Orbis Books, 1990.

Adegbola, Adeolu. "Christian Responsibility the Political Economy Africa." *The Ecumenical Review* 37 (January 1985): 86-97.

Aguilar, Delia D. *The Feminist Challenge: Initial Working Principles Toward Reconceptualizing the Feminist Movement in the Philippines*. Manila, Philippines: Asian Social Institute, 1988.

Appiah-Kubi, Kofi and Sergio Torres, Sergio, eds. *African Theology En Route*. Maryknoll, N.Y.: Orbis Books, 1979.

*Asian Women Doing Theology: Report from Singapore C o n f e r e n c e, November 20-29, 1987. Hong Kong:* Asian Women's Resource Centre for Culture and Theology, 1989.

Balasuriya, Tissa. *Planetary Theology*. Maryknoll, N.Y.: Orbis Books, 1984.

Bevans, Stephen. "Models of Contextual Theoology." *Missiology: An International Review* 13 (April 1985): 185-202.

Bimwenyi, O. K. "The Origins of EATWOT." *Voices from the Third World* 4 (December 1981): 19-26.

Bingemer, Maria Clara (Lucchetti). "Women in the Future of the Theology of Liberation." *In Expanding the View: Gustavo Gutierrez and the Future of Liberation Theology*, ed. Ellis, Marc H. and Otto Maduro, 173-193. Maryknoll, N.Y.: Orbis Books, 1990.

Boff, Leonardo. *The Maternal Face of God: The Feminine and Its Religious Expressions*. London: Collins Religious Publications, 1989.

Boff, Leonardo and Virgil Elizondo, eds. *Theologies of the Third World: Convergences and Differences,* Concilium. Edinburgh: T. & T. Clark Ltd., 1988.

Chapman, Cynthia R. "A Comparison of Gordon Kaufman's Christology with Those of Asian Feminists." *Ching Feng* 34 (September 1991): 154-167.

Chung, Hyun Kyung. *Struggle to Be the Sun Again: Introducing A s ia n Women's Theology*. Maryknoll, N.Y.: Orbis Books, 1990.

*Commemorating Amsterdam 1948: 40 Years of the World Council of Churches. The Ecumenical Review* 40 (July-October 1988).

Cone, James. *Black Theology and Black Power*. New York: Seabury Press, 1970.

————. "Ecumenical Association of Third World Theologians." *Ecumenical Trends* 14 (September 1985): 119-122.

Cormie, Lee. "Report on EATWOT Conference," *The Ecumenist* 21 (May-June 1983): 73-80.

Dussel, Enrique. "Theologies of the `Periphery' and the `Centre': Encounter or Confrontation?" *In Different Theologies, Common Responsibility: Babel or Pentecost?* ed. Claude Geffre, Gustavo Gutierrez, and Virgil Elizondo, 87-97. Concilium, T. & T. Clark Ltd., 1984.

*Everyone's United Nations,* 9th ed., New York: United Nations Publications, 1979.

Fabella, Virginia. "Emerging Third World Theologies." *Kalinangan* 3 (September 1983): 14-17, 20-21.

Fabella, Virginia, ed. *Asia's Struggle for Full Humanity*. Maryknoll, N.Y.: Orbis Books, 1980.

Fabella, Virginia and Dolorita Martinez, eds. *The Oaxtepec Encounter: Third World Women Doing Theology*. Ecumenical Association of Third World Theologians, n.d.

Fabella, Virginia, Peter K. H, Lee, and David Kwang-Sun Suh, eds. *Asian*

*Christian Spirituality: Reclaiming   Traditions.* Maryknoll, N.Y.: Orbis Books, 1992.

Fabella, Virginia and Sun Ai Lee Park, eds. *We Dare to Dream: Doing Theology as Asian Women.* Hong Kong: Asian Women's Resource Centre for Culture and Theology, 1989; Manila: The EATWOT Women's Commission in Asia, 1989.

Fabella, Virginia and Mercy Amba Oduyoye, eds. *With Passion and Compassion: Third World Women Doing Theology.* Maryknoll, N.Y.: Orbis Books, 1988.

Fabella, Virginia and Sergio Torres, eds. *Doing Theology in a Divided World.* Maryknoll, N.Y.: Orbis Books, 1985.

_____. *Irruption of the Third World: Challenge to Theology.* Maryknoll, N.Y.: Orbis Books, 1983.

"Feminine Voices in Asian Theology: Selected Papers from the Asian Women's Consultation, Manila, 21-30 November 1985," *Pro Mundi Vita: Dossiers* 4 (1986).

Gebara, Ivone, and Maria Clara Bingemer. *Mary: Mother of God, Mother of the Poor.* Maryknoll, N.Y.: Orbis Books,  1989.

Gnanadason, Aruna. "An Asian Feminine Response to EATWOT Statements from Dar Es Salaam to Mexico." *Voices from the Third World* 12 (June 1989): 1-13.

_____. "Indian Women: New Voices, New Visions." In *Third  W o r l d Theologies in Dialogue: Essays in Memory of D. S.  Amalorpavadass*, ed. J. Russell Chandran, 143—151. Ecumenical Association of Third World Theologians (EATWOT), 1991.

_____, ed. *Towards a Theology of Humanhood: Women's Perspectives.* Delhi: I.S.P.C.K. for the All India  Council of Christian Women, 1986.

Grimm, William J. "The `Third' World." *America* 162 (May 5, 1990): 449-451.

Gutierrez, Gustavo. *A Theology of Liberation.* 15th anniversary ed. Maryknoll, N.Y.: Orbis Books, 1988.

Henriot, Peter J., Edward P. DeBerri, and Michael J. Schultheis. "The Medellin Conference Documents." Chap. in *Catholic Social Teaching: Our Best Kept Secret.* Maryknoll, N.Y.: Orbis Books, 1985; Melbourne:

Dove Communications, 1985; Washington, D.C.: Center of Concern, 1985.

"In Search of a Filipino Women's Hermeneutical Principle." *Pintig Diwa Faculty Journal* 10 (October 1989): 1-12.

*In God's Image*. Quarterly journale published by the Asian Women's Resource Centre for Culture and Theoloigy, Hong Kong.

"Introduction," in *Reweaving the World: The Emergence of Ecofeminism,* with essays by the editors, ed. Irene Diamond and Gloria Feman Orenstein, ix-xv. San Francisco: Sierra Club Books, 1990.

Isasi-Diaz, Ada-Maria. *"Mujeristas*: A Name of Our Own." In *The Future ofLiberation Theology: Essays in Honor of Gustavo Gutierrez*, ed. Marc H. Ellis and Otto Maduro, 410-419. Maryknoll, N.Y.: Orbis Books, 1989.

Katoppo, Marianne. *Compassionate and Free: An Asian Woman's Theology*. Geneva, Switzerland: World Council of Churches, 1979.

Kwok, Pui-lan. *Chinese Women and Christianity 1860-1927*. Atlanta: Scholars Press, 1992.

_____. "Discovering the Bible in the Non-Biblical World." *Semeia* 47 (1989): 25-42.

Lee Park, Sun Ai. "Envisioning a Future Church as an Asian Woman." *Voices from the Third World* 12 (June 1989): 64-94.

Leny Lagerwerf, "African Women Doing Theology—A Survey." *Exchange* 19:1 (April 1990): 1-69.

Lerner, Gerda. *The Creation of Patriarchy*. Pp. 15-53. New York: Oxford University Press, 1986.

Lernoux, Penny. "The Long Path to Puebla." In *Puebla and Beyond*. ed. John Eagleson and Philip Scharper. Maryknoll, N.Y.: Orbis Books, 1979.

Mananzan, Mary John. "Emerging Spirituality Among Religious in the Philippines." In *Prophets for the Third Millennium*. First Religious Life Week, 135-152. Quezon City, Philippines: Claretian Publications, 1990.

_____. "Theological Perspectives of a Religious Woman Today." In *The*

*Future of Liberation Theology: Essays in Honor of Gustavo Gutierrez,* ed. Marc H. Ellis and Otto Maduro, 420-432. Maryknoll, N.Y.: Orbis Books, 1989.

McFague, Sallie. *Models of God: Theology for an Ecological, Nuclear Age.* Philadelphia: Fortress Press, 1987.

Nauta, Rommie and Klein Goldewijk, "Feminist Perspective in Latin American Liberation Theology." *Exchange* 48 (December 1987): 1-32.

O'Brien, David J. and Thomas A. Shannon, eds. *Renewing the Earth.* Garden City, N.Y.: Image Books, 1977.

Oduyoye, Mercy Amba. "A Biennial Institutes of African Women in Religion and Culture." *AMKA* 1 (1991): 7-10.

_____. *Hearing and Knowing: Theological Reflections on Christianity in Africa.* Maryknoll, N.Y.: Orbis Books, 1986.

_____. "`Image the Image of God...': A Theological Reflection from an African Perspective." *Bulletin of African Theology* 4, 7 (January-June 1982): 41-53.

_____. "Naming the Woman: The Words of the Akan and the Words of the Bible." *Bulletin of African Theology* 3, 5 (January-June 1981): 81-97.

_____. "Where are We in the EATWOT: Impressions of the Fifth Meeting Held in New Delhi, August 1981." In *Towards a Dialogue with Third World Theologians (1981),* ed. Jacques Van Nieuwenhove and Georges Casalis, 164-168. Zeist, The Netherlands: "Woudschoten," 1981.

Oduyoye, Mercy Amba, and Musimbi (R. A.) Kanyoro, eds. *Talitha, qumi! Proceedings of the Convocation of African Women Theologians, Trinity College, Legon-Accra, September 24-October 2, 1989.* Ibadan, Nigeria: Daystar Press, 1990.

_____. *The Will to Arise: Women, Tradition, and the Church in Africa.* Maryknoll, N.Y.: Orbis Books, 1992.

Okure, Teresa. "Biblical Perspectives on Women: Eve, the Mother of All." *Voices from the Third World,* Philippine edition, 8 (December 1985): 17-24.

Pieris, Aloysius, SJ. *An Asian Theology of Liberation.* Maryknoll, N.Y.: Orbis

Books, 1988.

Pobee, John S. and Von Wartenberg-Potter, Barbel, eds. *New Eyes for Reading: Biblical and Theological Reflections by Women from the Third World*. San Francisco: Harper Publishers, 1984.

"Proceedings: Asian Women's Consultation," Manila, November 21-30, 1985. Bound mimeographed.

*Rapport General: Consultation pour l'Afrique Francophone, Yaounde, 3-9 Aout, 1986*. Bound mimeographed.

Rayan, Samuel. "The Irruption of the Third World - A Challenge to Theology." *Vidyajyoti* (March 1982): 106-127.

Ruether, Rosemary Radford. *Sexism and God-Talk: Toward a Feminist Theology*. Boston: Beacon Press, 1983.

Russell, Letty M. *Household of Freedom: Authority in Feminist Theology*. Philadelphia: The Westminster Press, 1987.

_____, ed. *Feminist Interpretation of the Bible*. Philadelphia: The Westminster Press, 1985.

Russell, Letty M., Kwok Pui-lan, Ada Maria Isasi-Diaz, Katie Geneva Cannon, eds. *Inheriting Our Mothers' Garden: Feminist Theology in Third World Perspective*. Philadelphia: Westminster Press, 1988.

Schussler Fiorenza, Elisabeth. *Bread Not Stone: The Challenge of Feminist Biblical Interpretation*. Boston: Beacon Press, 1984.

_____. *In Memory of Her: A Feminist Theological Reconstruction of Christian Origins*. New York: The Crossroad Publishing Company, 1983.

Segundo, Juan Luis. *The Liberation of Theology*. Maryknoll, N.Y.: Orbis Books, 1976.

Shiva, Vandana. "Development as a New Project of Western Patriarchy." In *Reweaving the World: The Emergence of Ecofeminism*, with essays by the editors, ed. Irene Diamond and Gloria Feman Orenstein, 189-200. San Francisco: Sierra Club Books, 1990.

Tamez, Elsa. *Against Machismo*. Oak Park: Meyer Stone Books, 1987.

_____. *Bible of the Oppressed*. Maryknoll, N.Y.: Orbis Books, 1982.

_____, ed. *Las mujeres toman la palabra: entrevistas*. San Jose, Costa Rica: Editorial Departamento Ecumenico de Investigaciones (DEI), 1989.

_____, ed. *Through Her Eyes: Women's Theology from Latin America*. Maryknoll, N.Y.: Orbis Books, 1989.

Theological Education Fund. *Ministry in Context*. London: TEF, 1972.

Thistlethwaite, Susan Brooks. "On the Trinity." *Interpretation* 45/2 (April 1991): 159-171.

Torres, Sergio and Virginia Fabella, eds. *The Emergent Gospel: Theology from the Underside of History*. Maryknoll, N.Y.: Orbis Books, 1978.

Torres, Sergio and John Eagleson, eds. *The Challenge of Basic Christian Communities*. Maryknoll, N.Y.: Orbis Books, 1981.

_____. *Theology in the Americas*. Maryknoll, N.Y.: Orbis Books, 1976.

Trible, Phyllis. "An Unnamed Woman: The Extravagance of Violence." Chap. in *Texts of Terror*. Philadelphia: Fortress Press, 1984.

*Voices from the Third World*. Semi-annual bulletin published by the Ecumenical Association of Third World Theologians, 281 Deans Road, Colombo 10, Sri Lanka.

Weidman, Judith, ed. *Christian Feminism: Visions for a New Humanity*. San Francisco: Harper & Row, 1984.

Williams, "Womanist Theology: Black Women's Voices." *Christianity and Crisis* (March 2, 1987): 66-70.

## II. Other Sources

"Asian Women Theologians' Meeting: December 1990, Madras: Statement." Unpublished statement. Author's collection.

Bingemer, Maria Clara Lucchetti. Interview by author. September 30, 1989, Amsterdam, Netherlands. Tape recording.

"The Critical Hermeneutical Principles of Korean Women Theologians."

Unpublished paper written for the Asian Women Theologians' Meeting, December 15-20, 1990, Madras, India. Author's collection.

Fabella, Virginia. "A Theological Framework for the Woman Question." Unpublished paper written for the annual convention of the Association of Major Religious Superiors of Women in the Philippines, Tagaytay City, January 28, 1990. Author's collection.

"Final Communique: Consultation between Third World Women in the Third World Contexts and Third World Women in the First World Contexts." Unpublished statement marked "Not for public distribution." Author's collection.

Gnanadason, Aruna. Interview by author. December 31, 1990, Madras, India. Tape recording.

Kwok, Pui-lan. Interview by author. December 17, 1990, Madras, India. Tape recording.

_____. "Feminist Hermeneutics from a Chinese Perspective." Unpublished paper written for the Asian Women Theologians' Meeting, December 15-20, 1990, Madras, India. Author's collection.

Lee Park, Sun Ai. Interview by author. November 1, 1989, Kuala Lumpur, Malaysia. Tape recording.

Mananzan, Mary John. Interview by author. November 12, 1989, Manila, Philippines. Tape recording.

Oduyoye, Mercy Amba. Interview by author. October 3, 1989, Geneva, Switzerland. Tape recording.

_____. "Women's Critique of EATWOT: The African Continent." Unpublished paper written for the EATWOT General Assembly, Oaxtepec, Mexico, December 7-14, 1986. Oaxtepec (Second Five-Year Term), EATWOT Archives.

Okure, Teresa. Interview by author. September 29, 1989, Amsterdam, Netherlands. Tape recording.

Samuelson, Robert J. "End of the Third World." *Newsweek* July 30, 1990, 4.

Tamez, Elsa. Interview by author. October 4, 1989, Geneva, Switzerland. Tape recording.

_____. *"Informe de la reunion de teologia latinoamericana desde la perspectiva de la mujer."* Unpublished report submitted to the Executive Committee. Women's Commission (Second Five-year Term), EATWOT Archives.

Tapia, Elizabeth. "The Contribution of Philippine Christian Women to Asian Women's Theology." Ph.D. diss., Claremont Graduate School, Claremont, Calif, 1989.

Unpublished papers. Dar es Salaam Conference (First Five-year Term), EATWOT Archives.

Unpublished papers. Delhi Conference (First Five-year Term), EATWOT Archives.

Unpublished papers. International Women's Conference (Second Five-year Term), EATWOT Archives.

Unpublished papers. Oaxtepec Conference (Second Five-year Term), EATWOT Archives.

## ABOUT THE AUTHOR
◆ ◆ ◆

VIRGINIA FABELLA is uniquely suited to write the story of the women's theological journey within the Ecumenical Association of Third World Theologians (EATWOT). Besides being involved with the Association for over fifteen years and serving as its first woman executive secretary, Fabella was a key architect of its Women's Commission, actively participated in the Commission's programs and activities, and co-edited two collections of EATWOT and other Third World women's writings. Very importantly, she knew most of the women members of EATWOT personally.

As a Maryknoll Sister born in the Philippines, Fabella's assignments include not only the ecumenical ministry within EATWOT, but also missionary involvement in Latin America. She also taught in a women's college in Quezon City, Philippines and served as Director of the Maryknoll Sisters' Mission Institute in New York. At present, she is Academic Dean of the Institute of Formation and Religious Studies back in the Philippines.

Among the books on EATWOT which Fabella edited or co-edited are: *Emergent Gospel* (1978), *Asia's Struggle for Full Humanity* (1980), *Irruption of the Third World* (1983), *Doing Theology in a Divided World* (1985), *With Passion and Compassion* (1988), *We Dare to Dream* (1989), and *Asian Christian Spirituality* (1992).